VOLUME 3

WE ALL WANT TO BE HAPPY

A BOOK OF THOUGHTS

VOLUME 3

ANN MULLEN-MARTIN

We All Want to Be Happy: A Book of Thoughts (Volume 3)
Published by Annmuma Publishing
Mesquite, Texas, U.S.A.

MULLEN, ANN, Author
WE ALL WANT TO BE HAPPY (Volume 3)
ANN MULLEN

Library of Congress Control Number: 2025924377

ISBN: 979-8-9920093-2-3, 979-8-9920093-4-7 (paperback)
ISBN: 979-8-9920093-5-4 (hardcover)
ISBN: 979-8-9920093-3-0 (digital)

BIOGRAPHY & AUTOBIOGRAPHY / Women
SELF-HELP / Personal Growth / Happiness
BODY, MIND & SPIRIT / Inspiration & Personal Growth

Editing and Writing Coach: Nina Marshall (ramadevinina@yahoo.com)
Editing: Katie Chambers (beaconpointservices.org)
Book Design: Michelle M. White (mmwbooks.com)
Publishing Management: Tim Jacobs (jacobswc.com)
Publishing Consulting: Susie Schaefer (finishthebookpublishing.com)

I have dedicated more than one book to my brother,
John B. Yeager, Jr. I cannot think of anyone who
impacted my life more than John between the years of
1957 and 1961. I often envied his courage then,
and I still do today. It takes more than courage to
not only study yourself, but to embrace who you are and to
live in a place of peace. It also takes strong character, honesty,
and an acceptance of a universal truth: every person has
an assigned path to follow while on this earth.
I love you, John, and am so blessed because you are my brother.

~Ann Mullen-Martin

CONTENTS

FOREWORD

Although these stories are fictional, they are based on a real life I observed. I've changed a handful of names and locations to respect both the story and the characters.

To set the scene, let's meet the young man featured in the tales. On October 25, 1956, he was the apple of his mother's eye and the youngest son. The entire world seemed to be his oyster. On October 26, 1956, at the age of ten years, one month, and twenty-eight days, he lost his mother. Although his mother physically left this world, his memory of her and their relationship formed the framework by which John judged himself and others.

Losing a mom at any age is horrific. It's even more so for a boy drifting between being a child and moving toward pre-teen pressures. At not-yet-eleven years old, he navigated an upside-down and non-nurturing world. He fought daily to determine his place and find peace again. He dropped out of high school and went to California to live with a relative. On the day his age made him eligible, his father signed his permission slip to enlist in the army.

This book begins with Thanksgiving Day in November of 1963 and focuses on who John was and who he wanted to be.

The next section continues his journey. On March 10, 1964, a lonely and lost nineteen-year-old John received a medical discharge from the army. With travel pay in his pocket and no real goal in mind, he stumbled into whatever tomorrow would bring.

In 1966 he faced another life-changing event as a married father, facing the same transformation of becoming a complete adult that we all encounter. Money was now important, but John was not quite ready to give up all his playtime. During the years covered in the concluding section, he took a successful step toward developing his character with a sense of what is profoundly important and necessary for the best life:

PEACE OF MIND

CHAPTER
ONE

Thanksgiving, 1963

In November 1963, as turmoil and unrest engulfed the United States, John—like most of us at that time—gathered up his positivity, put on his best smile, and approached the holiday season with the hope of finding peace within himself. The Cuban Missile Crisis left us all with a feeling of unease. President John F. Kennedy's assassination in Dallas, Texas, threw the entire country into mourning.

Still, being Americans, John's fellow soldiers at Fort Polk made plans for the day—many to spend time in the area with families who had become friends in recent months. John sat on his bunk listening to the others. The recent assassination generated extra time and some extra money for those leaving the military. Although his discharge money wasn't accessible in his wallet, but rather was somewhere embroiled in a payroll snafu, he began to daydream about a family Thanksgiving.

Raining and forty-five degrees? But Tioga's only sixty-five miles away. With a couple of lucky rides . . . I'm good at hitchhiking and may see some people I haven't seen in a while.

All he knew was he had to get out. He needed to go. What he was really searching for was the need to feel the love and specialness of just being himself. He grabbed his backpack and strolled out the gate and to the highway. He prepared himself for a long wait, but like unexpected rain on a sunny day, an old pickup slowed to a stop at about the same time that he put out his thumb.

"Hey, looking for a ride?"

"Yessir. I need to head south a bit."

"Hop in."

Once they had introduced themselves, the driver continued to talk, glancing over at John every now and then.

"You know, John, I've been right where you are now. Holiday leave. I'll never forget the feeling of walking into my mama's warm house. Yeah, what a day to remember! Everybody hugged me and told me I was some kind of hero. I never even made it to Korea, but that didn't matter. Now, here you're gonna surprise your folks, are you? That'll be something!"

John listened and nodded. The Leesville city limits sign came into view, and the driver signaled he would not be going any farther as he refueled his vehicle. John smiled and offered a handshake before sauntering into the gas station to visit the bathroom and get something to drink. While he waited for the rain to let up a bit, he leaned on the counter and talked with the clerk. About an hour passed before he stepped back out into the wind, trying to avoid the rain that had not let up. Standing at the outside edge of the gas pump canopy did little to protect a dripping wet and shivering John from the elements.

His feeling of good fortune rebounded when another driver, gassing up, appeared to be leaving and then made a turn back toward John.

"Need a ride?"

"Yessir, I do. Trying to get to Kingsville."

As the driver opened the door, he looked John up and down. "Been on the road long?"

"No, sir. Just coming in from Fort Polk."

He handed John a beer. "Well, climb in. Let's see if I can get you a little closer."

John thanked him for the beer with a smile as he settled into the front seat. This guy leaned to the quiet side. He turned up the heater a notch and freely shared his beer, making the ride to Billips Café in Kingsville even more pleasant. Although the wind had calmed, the rain continued to vary between a downpour and a sprinkle. Without considering any other options, John headed in the direction of his grandfather's house. With not a ride to be had, he walked in the rain every inch of the six long miles.

Upon arrival, he stood there for a few minutes, staring at the long driveway from a distance. His shoes were squishy, with his socks saturated and now down to the middle of his feet, exposing blisters to both ankles. The tin-roofed house looked a mile away, and his thoughts wandered to an earlier time in his life when, too many times to count, he had depended on his grandpa to get him through one more day. Just the thought brought a layer of peace as he visualized those visits, each one of them almost a carbon copy of the others. Arriving home—almost home, anyway—felt as warm as standing in front of a fireplace after coming in from the cold. A typical scene replayed in his mind:

He would climb down from the horse he had ridden, and his grandpa would be there to greet him with a grin.

"Hey, boy. Want some coffee?"

"Yessir! Let me put my horse up."

He liked to sit and stare at his grandpa. To him, the large and confident man personified a warm blanket of unconditional love. His presence created a cloud of safety, security, and freedom. He never felt more guarded and invincible than he did when nestled in his grandpa's refuge of acceptance. Today, the sound of his grandpa's voice as he reached the house quickly replaced the nostalgia with reality.

"Hey, boy. You want some coffee?" Grandpa met him and stuck out his hand as if he were expecting him, as he always did. The touch contained palpable unconditional love, which John needed, whether he was aware of it or not.

"Yessir."

Just hearing Grandpa's voice and feeling his hand on his shoulder temporarily calmed the storm that quietly raged in his mind, that aching need. His grandpa's chuckle became a lighthouse beam shining through his fog of confusion, leading his mind-ship to safe port. John relaxed with a sigh and a smile.

"Grace. Johnny's here. Put on a pot of coffee," Grandpa yelled back through the door before he sat down on the porch, put the end of his pipe in his mouth and leaned the chair against the wall—an admirable feat. The chair touched the wall at such an angle that the back two legs, the only ones supporting the chair, rested solely on their back rims.

John stood, anticipating his grandpa's next attempt at humor.

"Looks like you're a bit wet. I didn't even notice it was raining." With that, he laughed and adjusted his pipe once again.

John continued to stand.

"Know what, boy? I think we oughta go on in the house and sit in front of the fire a bit."

A smile crossed John's face, and he had the screen door open before his grandpa could get out of his chair and avoid a fall at the same time. Settled into a rocking chair in front of the fireplace, John laughed again at Grandpa's joke. He loved the sound of his grandfather's laugh and his sense of humor; indeed, Grandpa enjoyed his own humor at least as much as his listeners did.

Like a good fairy, Grace seemed to appear out of thin air, holding two steaming cups of coffee and wearing a welcoming smile. "You're staying for dinner." She made it more of a statement than a question. She placed the mugs down, pivoted and returned to the kitchen without awaiting an answer.

John leaned back in his chair, listening to the rain on the tin roof and enjoying the good smells drifting through the house. He and his grandfather looked at each other fondly, sharing the understanding of their special relationship.

"How long you got, Johnny?"

"Probably go back tomorrow evening. I guess I could stay through the weekend—not likely."

"Gonna be eating dinner in a little while."

"Sure smells good."

"Well, hope you'll eat with us."

As the silence settled in again, he heard Grace talking to one of the twins. "Poor little Johnny. Guess he don't have anywhere else to go for Thanksgiving. Be sure to set him a plate."

John didn't have any deep feelings for his mom's stepmother. She had always been good to him, but he saw her as nothing more than Grandpa's wife. He couldn't explain why, but her words cut him to the bone. That warm, comfortable feeling disappeared, and an unreasonable false pride rose up. He spoke louder than necessary as he stood up.

"Grandpa, I don't have time to eat. I've got so many places to go. If I don't get started, I'm bound to miss somebody who's waiting to see me."

"Johnny, sit down. I hate seeing you go. We'll be eating in minutes."

"I wish I could stay, but I just can't." He fought back tears.

While Grandpa's invitation had been sincere, he also accepted John's response. He always accepted John and his sudden decisions; he didn't understand them, but he accepted them. They shook hands, then Grandpa walked him to the porch and down the steps. John cried unacknowledged tears that dripped slowly as they walked toward the gate.

"Stay dry, boy."

"I'll try, Grandpa."

They both laughed as Grandpa patted him on the back, then stood, hands on hips. John waved as he ambled down the long driveway and turned south when it met the highway. Grandpa returned to the fireplace, lost in memory of so many good times watching Johnny grow.

Meanwhile, John stuck out his thumb and, within minutes, shared a Ford pickup cab with another kind soul heading in the direction of Alexandria. The same small talk that begins every hitched ride created the background for John's thoughts.

"Where are you headed?"

"Alexandria."

"Awful wet Thanksgiving Day to be on the road."

"Yeah, guess so."

John barely heard the driver speaking as he considered where he might go. He thought about the E&E Club on upper Third Street. His half-brother had introduced him to the E&E well before his sixteenth birthday. As he mulled over the Saturday nights he had wasted there, he imagined faces from the past. He might even be able to swing a beer or two. He glanced out the window and realized they were within just a mile or so of the E&E.

"Hey, buddy. Let me out right here."

"Listen, I'm happy to take you wherever you're going."

"This is close enough. I'll walk from here."

"You sure?" the driver asked one last time as he slowed to a stop.

"Yeah. Thanks." John opened the door and hopped out without saying another word. He didn't want this total stranger to know where he was going, but for his life, he didn't know why. He stuck his hands in his pockets, ducked his head a little to keep the sprinkling rain out of his eyes and, with an added jaunt to his step, walked toward the E&E Club.

Just as it came into sight, he read the "Closed for Thanksgiving" sign, and his spirits tumbled. A weird and long-ago memory burst in crystal clear: asking for a bike for Christmas and getting plastic toy soldiers instead. Strangely, the thought brought a smile. His half-brother lived in a rooming house just a couple of blocks over.

With his best swagger, he headed for Ninth and Beauregard. Although he thought Henry might be out at their dad's, he knew the landlady pretty well. She might be good afternoon company. With that thought in mind, he rang the doorbell. All smiles, the landlady opened the door.

"Well, Johnny! What a surprise. I bet you're looking for Henry. He just left, went down to the café. Come on in," she said, all in one breath and with the added welcome of an arm on his shoulder. "Come on in," she repeated and added a squeeze for emphasis.

John briefly hesitated before crossing the threshold.

"Let me get you something dry! Only take a minute." She left the room, returning with what must have been one of Henry's shirts and a jacket.

"Boy, that feels good! I didn't know how cold I was." They both laughed as she folded the freshly dried military gear into a plastic bag. Neither sat down. "I sure appreciate this, Rose. I gotta get on over to see Henry. You say he's at the café?"

"I can't imagine he's anywhere else, Johnny. He said something about going out to his dad's, but not until tomorrow."

John picked up the plastic bag, gave her a hug, and left her standing on the porch, waving and watching him leave.

Henry only went to two restaurants: the Majestic and the Double V, catty-corner to the Majestic. Mrs. Moreni ran the Majestic, and she knew John well.

"I didn't know you were in town, Johnny. If you're looking for Henry, he's across the street at the Double V, playing pinball."

John said not a word as he made a U-turn out of the café. Within a couple of minutes, he located Henry on a barstool, propped up on the bar with a Falstaff in front of him. At a tap on his shoulder, Henry turned around.

"Hey, Johnny! When did cha roll in?" Without waiting for an answer, he motioned to the bartender. "Bring my brother a beer over here."

With the ease of putting on an old shoe, they fell back into familiar banter about nothing. Several minutes later, John broached the subject of Thanksgiving.

"Whatcha doing for Thanksgiving?"

"You see it! I'm drinking my Thanksgiving. I was short this week; had to roll my note. Still owed'em twenty bucks, but they lemme me have eighty anyway. At ten bucks a week, I only hafta pay back a hundred and twenty. Really, not bad." Henry stared at his beer, and John stared at him.

"You got any of that eighty left?"

"Yeah, sure, maybe fifty, maybe sixty. Why?" He lit up a Winston and threw the pack on the bar. "Wanna cigarette? How 'bout another beer?"

"Yeah, I could use another beer," John said as he lit a cigarette. "But I'm broke. Think my check is still somewhere in Germany." Though it made no sense at all, both men laughed as if it were the best joke of the day.

"Makes no never mind, Johnny. This one's on me."

They shared a couple more beers and talked about how things were going at the lumber yard where Henry worked. Slowly, a dark, wet cloud of depression settled in over John. A chill ran up his spine. Henry's stories were as worn and sad as an old homeless guy talking about the good old days. Shaking it off, he stood up, reached for his military shirt that the landlady had so kindly dried for him, and clapped Henry on the back.

"Gotta get outta here, man."

"Where're you going?"

"Tioga. Gonna check in with Daddy. I guess he's home?"

"Yeah. Guess so. Tell him I'm coming out tomorrow. Not sure he worked today or not; you know how he is about trying to work every holiday!"

They shared one more laugh over their unusual father. He handed John two dollars. "This oughta getcha home."

John's hitchhiking luck held, and he caught a ride almost immediately. By three thirty, he stood at his father's front screen door. He watched his dad, clad in his usual overalls, sleeping in a rocking chair in front of a heater where the fireplace had once been. Having slid down into the chair, Dad rested with his legs splayed out and his arms folded across his stomach. His chin rested on his chest, and his glasses sat about halfway down his nose. John felt a pang of loneliness, as if lightning had hit him dead center in his heart.

He quickly knocked, and his dad awakened immediately.

"Come on in, boy. I didn't know you were in town." He spoke as he got up to open the door. "What are you doing home?"

"Got extra leave time 'cause of Kennedy."

"I think the wrong Kennedy was shot. Have you been out to Grandpa's yet?"

They returned to the rocking chairs facing the heater.

"Yeah. They invited me to dinner, but I wanted to see Henry and get by here. By the way, Henry will be out tomorrow."

"You should've eaten at Grandpa's."

"What are you doin' Daddy? For Thanksgiving?"

His dad chuckled, rolling his cheek between his thumb and forefinger as John had seen him do a thousand times when he was not sure of what he was going to say. "Well, nothing."

That short statement set off nearly an hour of just sitting next to each other. Then his dad broke the silence. "Have you eaten anything today?"

"Oh, yeah. I stopped in Alex after I said hello to Henry." He was always careful to be sure his dad believed him to be self-sufficient. Some people might call that lying; John called it the price he paid to gain stature in his father's eyes.

"Then you've already eaten?"

"Yeah. Sure have. What about you?"

His dad changed the subject to his latest dog, Spike, and then to Butch, a dog John had before he joined the army. Probably thirty minutes passed in conversation, and John had about given up on the possibility of eating when, without any lead-in, his dad said, "You think you could eat a hamburger?"

John's stomach did a double lurch, and he could almost taste it. "Yeah. Maybe a burger. It's been a while since I ate back in Alex—and a very long time since I had a Billips hamburger."

"Let me get my shoes, and we'll take a ride over there."

At Billips, the hamburger patties were on the grill, two truck drivers sat at the counter and a couple of people that his dad knew sat at the tables. They exchanged hellos and handshakes all around. Everybody agreed they each had their health to be thankful for, and John and his dad settled in at a table. The waitress materialized as quickly as a genie out of a magic lamp.

"Hey, Mr. Yeager. Good to see you. I see your boy's home?"

"Yeah, he is, Myrtle. How are you?" He reached for her hand, and John's face turned crimson. His dad loved to flirt with the ladies.

"I'm just thankful for my health on this cold, rainy Thanksgiving Day. What can I bring you?"

"Bring that boy a hamburger. No, wait a minute." He turned to John. "Think you could eat two?"

John grinned. "I could sure try!"

"Bring the boy two burgers, double fries and a Grapette to go with 'em." He teased the waitress, carried on a bit, and John got his hamburgers.

While John ate, his dad walked around, visiting everyone, including another truck driver passing through and a couple of guys who looked like hitch-hikers. After John downed the last bite of burgers, his dad tipped the waitress two bucks, and they were out the door. A quiet, comfortable silence settled over his dad's car as they rode home.

A million thoughts and memories flooded John's mind, and he knew what his dad's first words would be before he turned off the motor at the front gate.

As they got out of the car, his dad asked, "Son, how long you think you might be staying with me? Got weekend plans?"

The words were exactly what he expected, and he couldn't suppress a chuckle. "Thought I'd stay the night here at the house. Henry's catching a bus out in the morning."

"When do you need to report at Fort Polk?"

"Well, I got the whole weekend, but you know how I like to get home early." John swallowed hard. *Why didn't I stop after "I got the whole weekend"?* Maybe he just wanted to give his dad an out for anything he might say. Perhaps his dad would ask him to stay the whole weekend, but that wasn't his daddy's way. He just said, "Okay," and mounted the steps. Once inside, his dad turned the TV on to catch the news, which evoked little conversation. By seven thirty, the TV was off.

"Son, I think it's about time for bed. When you work, bedtime comes early. Why don't you crawl into the bed in Henry's room?"

Although he had lived in that house since he was four years old, he had never been assigned a bedroom. Henry, who only came out maybe a couple of weekends a month and had never lived in the house, had ownership. There were two more bedrooms, and they belonged to his dad and sisters. For just a minute, he felt almost lost, but quickly recovered; he was the youngest—the excuse he had heard his entire life for any slight he may have felt.

"Yessir. I think I'll do that." He spoke with a smile in his voice, and his dad reached over to briefly put his arm around him. "Good night, son. It's good to see you."

Hours of tossing and turning were followed by a brief sleep before he awoke to the smell of fresh coffee.

"That coffee ought to be about ready. Pour us both a cup," his dad said as John walked into the living room. The scene looked much as it had the night before, with his dad already settled into a rocking chair in front of the heater. "What's your plan for today?" he asked. "You know I have to be at work by three."

"Yeah, I know." John went to the kitchen, returned with two cups of coffee, and handed one to his dad. "Just like you like it! A half cup, black and hot."

After another hour of non-conversation and a couple more cups of coffee, his dad turned toward him, looking serious. "What time d'you reckon you'll be leaving? Your uniform looked a mess when you came in last night. You'll want to get that cleaned up. A man needs to look good before he shows up to work."

John nodded. Sure, he could ask to stay—he'd be welcome—but he couldn't form the words and didn't even know how to ask. His dad shared the same reluctance to reveal any personal feelings.

He took a deep breath and stood up. "You're right, Dad. I'll get my things together and be on my way." He extended his hand, and his dad stood to receive it. He gathered his uniform and his backpack and stood in front of his dad in less than an hour. His dad looked a little surprised as he stood to meet his gaze.

"You got any money, boy?"

"A little."

"How much is a little?"

"I'm running light. My separation check and leave payment got lost because of my transfers from Germany. I talked to somebody last week and learned the money should arrive in San Antonio—Brooke Army Medical Center at Fort Sam Houston. So, it'll catch up. Eventually!"

"You're not drinking up any checks, are you?"

"No, sir."

"Well, it's not the worst thing in the world to have money following you around." Both he and his dad laughed over that as his dad opened his overalls' breast pocket to retrieve his billfold.

"Here's a twenty. That should get you through to payday."

John's eyes clouded, and he looked down as they shook hands. He let go, walked out the door without looking back and was sitting on his bunk well before dark. After pulling out one of the books he had stored under the mattress, *Another Country* written by James Baldwin, he lay down to read until the evening mess hall SOS (shit on a shingle, the more common name for chopped beef in gravy on toast) meal was served.

He would not speak to his dad again until March 1964—after his separation money had reached him.

CHAPTER
TWO

Spreading the Word

On March 10, 1964, a nineteen-year-old John stood at the gates of Fort Polk, an Army post in Louisiana, newly discharged, with no future. His travel pay (based on getting back to Suisun City, California, where he initially enlisted) gave him extra dollars to spend while he made up his mind. He grabbed his duffel bag, threw it on his shoulder and put his thumb out for the backward shuffle south toward Alexandria.

He caught his first ride within a couple of miles from the base and settled in for a pleasant transport to his boyhood home. At around three that afternoon, he glimpsed the Tioga city limit sign in the distance.

"Hey, buddy, just drop me off here."

The truck driver looked over. "Thought you said you were heading for Baton Rouge."

"Never said that. Goin' to Alex. But I've changed my mind. My dad lives about a mile and a half down that road. Think I'll surprise him."

The trucker pulled over. John hopped out. With a wave, he started walking again. Money jingled in his pocket; the sun was shining and the lack of any plan felt good.

This is what real freedom feels like!

His dad's driveway led up a long hill, and for a few minutes, he stood at the cattle gap, allowing childhood memories to come rushing back. The house had not changed, and the same neighbors were next door. He saw and heard Spike, his dad's beloved dog, barking and running along the fence line. As he began the journey up the driveway, his dad appeared on the front porch, obviously headed for his car. He proceeded to drive down the drive and, about halfway, he met John on the way up.

"Hey, boy. Didn't know you were in town."

"Didn't expect to be, but I'm here."

"Well, I'm on my way to work. The house ain't locked. Go on up, and I'll see you later. I'll be in around midnight."

The car started rolling while he was still speaking. They had last seen each other four months ago, and while some would expect a little more emotion at a homecoming, that was not their relationship. They each waved as his dad drove off, and he continued up the hill to an empty house.

He enjoyed a month or so, visiting old friends, hanging out with his half-brother downtown, and just loafing, but soon his money and his dad's patience began to run short. One afternoon, the phone rang as he sat in a rocking chair, counting his last few one-dollar bills.

"Hello."

"Hey, John? Is that you? I didn't even know you were home!"

"Well, Olevia, I don't tell you everything, but I was about to call you. Daddy's got your number written right here, BR9-5985." He laughed, and his sister did as well.

"About what, John? I wish you would come over here. I want you to meet your new baby nephew, and you and Ronnie will really like each other."

"Just so happens that's what I was going to call you about."

"What?"

"Coming over there. I've visited with Daddy enough. Thought I might try Dallas. Daddy's been telling me there are no jobs in Tioga. Think maybe it's time I move on."

"Oh, John, I'm so excited. I'll come get you."

"No need for that. Just give me your address, and I'll see you in a few days."

"I'm coming down there."

With that, his sister's voice morphed into a dial tone. As an older sister, Olevia was a little hard-headed, always exercising the bossing rights she thought came with age. Anyway, he really did want her to come get him, but it felt better when it was not only her idea, but she insisted.

Expecting this to be his last night in Tioga, he called a buddy, and they turned his last twenty bucks into a good time.

The six-hour drive to Garland allowed Olevia to blather on with her disjointed and meandering dreams: Ronnie would get John a job. He would help around the house. What fun they would have. Like they were now one big happy family.

John's thoughts rambled in a different direction. He had talked to the employment office in Alexandria and knew he could draw checks for six months. His DD214 and an honorable discharge guaranteed the money would come rolling in. Thoughts of time off to get the lay of the land and enjoy life drowned out Olevia's incessant chatter.

The next day, John hitchhiked to the employment office and walked back to his sister's house to wait for that first check. He pulled off his shoes and became almost comfortable before his brother-in-law started talking about jobs. Working did not have a spot on John's six-month agenda, but life under someone else's roof did. So, he listened.

"John, I got a friend over at Republic Air Conditioning. Want me to talk to him about a job for you?"

"Well, I don't have to go to work right away, you know."

"If I talked to him, I bet you could start on the same day you showed up."

"That fast, huh?"

His brother-in-law paid no attention to the sarcasm, or maybe he just didn't notice. He plowed on. "I'm not kidding, and we can get you some kind of car to drive back and forth."

Before John could stop Ronnie from arranging it, he had a job and found himself in bumper-to-bumper traffic on his way down Inwood Boulevard to work on an assembly line at Republic Air Conditioning.

His job as a brake press operator didn't match his talents at all. But, suited for it or not, he drew $1.35 an hour making outside shells for air conditioners.

On the same day he began working, he started mapping his departure.

About two weeks into the hell of his job with Republic Air Conditioning, the lead man stopped by.

"Hey, John, you got a minute?"

"Don't know, Rosales. Leavin' this brake press unattended might be dangerous."

Rosales glared at him. Seemed like people in Dallas lacked a certain appreciation of humor. He followed Rosales to the back room.

"John, your brother-in-law's a good friend of mine. That's why you got this job."

"Really? I thought his friend was Walker in the front office."

"You need to understand I'm the guy you want to please. I decide who works here and who doesn't."

"Well, that sounds important. Congratulations. And this—"

"Come Christmas, we lay off most everybody. I decide who stays. You want to know how I decide?"

"Do you want to tell me?"

"Well, if a fellow brings me a cigar now and then, it goes in his favor. And I like Budweiser. When I'm making up that layoff list, I keep those things in mind."

This job had interrupted John's plan for a six-month vacation at the government's expense. A light went off in his brain.

"Rosales, when I buy beer, I'll be the one drinking it."

"I don't think you understand, John—"

John had heard all he wanted to hear. "Understand this." He walked past Rosales, punched out, picked up his lunch box and walked out.

Looking back now, he sees a smart-mouthed kid who lacked people skills, but on that day, he felt as if he had been named the heavyweight champion of the world. He picked up a six-pack, visited the employment office, and headed home with visions of sleeping in and staying up late.

Within days, his brother-in-law noticed that John seemed to be around the house too much.

"Hey, John. Are you still at Republic?"

Geez, I underestimated this guy. He has no idea who I am. Wonder how he came to have such an on-steroids work ethic. Maybe he just can't stand to see someone else not working. The Texas Employment Commission should hire him; the unemployment rate would be absolutely zero.

He kept those thoughts to himself and answered, "Nah. That's not the kind of job that suits me. Don't worry about it. I'm okay for a couple of months. I'll look around on my own."

"What did you do in the army?"

"I worked as a physician's assistant, at least that's what my DD214 says. Not sure you would want me helping the doctor who was helping you." He laughed as he tried to change the subject with a couple of jokes.

But again, Mr. Everybody Works pressed on. "Know what? I know a guy in the X-ray department down at St. Paul Hospital. I'll give him a call."

The interview didn't go that well, and John did nothing to encourage them to hire him, but within a week, his dream vacation had again become a distant goal. His new job involved taking X-rays with the only vocabulary needed: "Breathe, don't breathe. Okay, breathe."

Still, he liked the people and enjoyed the feeling of being helpful. But he simply could not come to terms with having a full-time job. He completed a month before he gave in to his need to visit his Louisiana gal again, a girl he got to know while visiting his dad. He had spent most of his weekends there, but when the money ran out, so did their interest in each other. But now he had money again. That fourth St. Paul Hospital check and his thumb got him to Colfax and the girl he remembered.

The end of their renewed relationship mirrored their earlier one: when the money ran out, he landed back in Dallas on Olevia's couch.

Well, not exactly on her couch. He sat across the kitchen table from "the employment specialist," who knew another thousand places eager to have John work for them. The whole scene made him sort of mad, as his chances of collecting unemployment were now blown. His brother-in-law never asked him to kick in on anything, never asked him to pay rent or buy groceries; in fact, he helped him buy a car. Ronnie's sole path to satisfaction seemed to be seeing John leave for work every day.

It was a bit weird, but the State of Texas does not pay someone if they repeatedly take jobs and quit. He had no money, and a job had become a necessity. Of course, there was one already lined up.

"John, go on down to Resistol, the hat factory. They're hiring, and I'm sure you can get on," Ronnie said.

"Why would I want to work at a hat factory?"

"Because you can't live here unless you work."

That came as a cold shock to John. If he had been left to his own devices, his *welfare check*—as Ronnie called it—could have contributed to the household. Paying for groceries and a bed filled John's requirements, but neither Olevia nor her husband had ever asked for a dime. His lack of a job grated on their nerves.

The Resistol hat factory was close to home, so there was no harm in taking a drive over. A tiny, old, red-haired woman met him at the door.

John put out his hand. "My brother-in-law said you are hiring. Are you?"

"Yes, sir, we are. What are you looking for?"

"Work."

Again, not a smile; no one seemed to appreciate his humor. She continued, "Today, I have a rack-pusher's job opening. It pays minimum wage."

"Are the racks heavy?"

Another attempt at humor wasted.

"No. A child could push them around. The secret is to satisfy the hatmakers by having the right supplies available at the right time."

"Well, ma'am, do you think I could do it?"

"Sure. It doesn't require much training to push racks." John wondered if she were making a joke now, but she didn't laugh. He stifled a chuckle.

"Come on back here, and I'll show you."

Resistol's hiring manager led John around the factory, introducing him to six women, five of whom reminded him of toads. And not just any toads—old toads, constipated toads, waiting for a fly to pass close enough to be hit by their sharp tongues. Their expressions mimicked one another, as if they all suffered from indigestion. Any one of the five would easily fill the bill as the wicked stepmother in any fairy tale. Despite attempting to hide their features under an inch or two of makeup, being disgruntled came through loud and clear. Similar guttural noises followed his introduction to each of them, and no one ever looked up from their work.

The sixth one was different.

"Hi. My name's Edith." She extended her hand.

Perfect, gleaming white teeth, shoulder-length blond hair, and no makeup at all set her apart. Her collar was buttoned. Her sleeves reached her wrists, and her skirt fell just below the knees. Her smile filled the room. In the absence of any romantic or physical feeling, given she was old enough to be his mother, her aura of niceness took hold of John. She radiated *goodness* or something close to it, and this, along with her chaste appearance, made him want to make a good impression.

He stuck out his hand, which she gratefully accepted.

"I'm John. Nice to meet you." A feeling of belonging enveloped his psyche as if he had found the puzzle piece to complete the project. This job could work out. Yep, he didn't need to quit. It would be good.

The voice of the hiring manager cracked his dream open. "You want this job? We've completed the factory tour, and if you take the job, I'm your supervisor."

"Yes, ma'am. I want to give it a try."

"You can start right now, if you want."

"I'm ready."

With an unknowing smile and unusual eagerness, an unsuspecting John took the first step into a new world.

* * *

Other than making minimum wage, he knew little else about the job, such as hours or benefits. Yet, he immediately felt like part of the team. The boss lady showed him a stack of hats and explained that the six women were paid based on production.

"The more of these hat linings they sew in, the more money they make. Your job's to keep 'em in hats. Watch while I show you the ropes." She picked up one hat to begin the demonstration.

"This one we call the eighty-nine. It's a typical hat, easy to work on, and the ladies finish these fast. Your job is to be certain these hats are distributed evenly. The rest of the hats are distributed in between the eighty-nines."

"What do you mean *evenly*?"

"Well, you always begin with the first lady. Give her a rack of these easy hats, and she doesn't get another one until you've gone completely around the horn. That's the way to keep everybody happy."

"What happens if one of them finishes a rack before it's her turn again?"

"John, just listen, and I'll explain it all." She sounded a little short, so he tuned in to the rest of her story.

"These number eighty-nines are called pass-outs, When one of them gets through trimming the regular hats they've been assigned, they will call out 'I need hats.' That's your signal to roll over a rack of these eighty-nines. When she finishes those, she begins another regular hat batch."

"Okay, I think I've got it: Everyone gets a set of pass-outs first; then a round of regular hats to set next to them. Both sets of hats must be finished before the next set of pass-outs—again with a rack of regulars. The ladies determine when they get their new supply by yelling 'I need hats.'

Sounds easy enough. Where do I start?"

She indicated with a nod of her head toward a sort of box-like station, almost hidden by racks of hats.

"That's where you stand. Every day."

The racks were one foot wide, about five feet tall and accommodated maybe fifteen hats, each hanging on a little wire. He reached the appointed spot in conjunction with one of the women yelling, "I need hats!"

Had his post been located down the block and two streets over, her yell would have reached him. He rushed over with a rack of eighty-nines and another of her next regular hat assignment. Despite the mental note he had formed regarding the pass-out rule, he made a couple of mistakes, which made it unforgettable from that day on.

"Hey, boy. Gimme those hats. It's not her turn. Pay 'tention to whacha doin'!" one woman yelled as if he were not standing less than five feet from her.

Another complained, "We're tryin' to make a livin'. Work with us."

A third one added, "The last person who had your job don't have it anymore. Know why? They couldn't keep up."

Those "toads" quickly morphed into a physical and mental man-eating mob filling the room like a thick gray smoke, stifling every ray of sunshine. John apologized, corrected his mistakes, and made a conscious decision to keep this job. Edith added a mellow tone to the whole atmosphere. Interaction with her included *please, thank you* and *I appreciate it.* She was the ray of sunshine John needed.

For reasons he could not explain, he knew this was where he belonged, at least for now; besides, he had grown tired of job hopping.

At lunch Edith invited him to join her and exhibited an interest in John in a mothering kind of way. Loss of his mom, years before, had left a hole in his heart that he rarely exposed to anyone. Edith's ease and easy acceptance of him breached that wall. Fifteen minutes before starting time each day, they stood chatting in the parking lot; they became regular lunch partners. He bared his soul to her and lapped up every word she said. A couple of weeks passed in their easy and open conversations before Edith posed the question that formed step two in his journey into uncharted territory.

* * *

"John, have you been saved?"

He stared for what felt like an eternity, searching for the right answer. His memory drifted back to a time when he fell into what he thought was quicksand. His friend, Chester, shared the disaster with him. They didn't know if it was really quicksand or not. It might have been sucking mud. Whatever it was, the fear still made his heartbeat fast as he recalled the incident. He and Chester had raced to the bottom of a gravel pit and that mud vacuum began to eat them alive.

"John, I can't lift my legs! I think I'm sinking. Are we being sucked into this mud?"

"Help!" John screamed.

They both continued to yell while a nearby schoolmate ran for help. It probably wasn't more than five minutes until he returned with two construction workers, but it felt endless. Even with the help of the men, the boys had fought the wet, sucking sand to save their lives. Every move seemed as if it might be their last. "Saved" certainly applied to that situation, and John shared the story with her. He trembled as he related every detail.

"Edith, I'm not sure I've ever shared this story with anybody. It still scares me, even though those construction guys saved our lives."

She listened to every word, fully engaged in the story. She didn't hurry him along or try to change the subject.

"Well, that must have been awful. What did you think about when death came so close?"

"One thing I thought was, at least I'll see Mama again in heaven." He smiled and relaxed a bit. Sharing that event with someone so kind and interested provided comfort comparable to the flame of small candle after a power outage had turned the room dark.

Edith returned his smile and touched his arm. "I'm glad you were saved from that mud pot so I could meet you today."

Although no answer was called for, he replied, "Thank you."

"But, John, that temporary saving is not what I mean. Have you ever met Jesus?"

He pondered that for a couple of minutes. His dad and mama believed in God, and he had spent his Sunday mornings in a Baptist church with his sisters when he was a kid. Mama was sick, and Daddy was often at work, although he did not go to church even if he was home. He dug deeper to be sure his answer came across as completely honest, not frivolous.

"No, not really. I mean, my family was a church-going family, but meeting Jesus? I don't think so."

"Well, we're having a revival down at my church, and I'd love you to come."

"What church is it?

"Assembly of God. I'm Holiness. Would you join me for an evening at the revival?"

"I don't know, Edith. My car's broke down again, and I don't think I can make it."

"I'll come get you."

"No, not a good idea. I need to stay around the house. My sister and her husband are about to go out of town and—"

"I have a really pretty little daughter. I'd like you to meet her."

An invitation to church, with a pretty girl attached.

That added a whole new dimension to the conversation. John had a girlfriend who lived in Louisiana. The last time he had gone to see her, it had cost him a job because he got too comfortable lying on her front porch swing. She was a nice enough girl—and pretty convenient, if you know what I mean. *What do they say nowadays? Friends with benefits.*

She was attached to him. Her mother liked him, and even her brother seemed to enjoy his company. But if he became part of that family, one day he would likely be its sole support, or maybe its sole *lack* of support. That didn't sit well with him, so meeting a new girl might just take his mind off Louisiana.

"Yeah, Edith, I wanna come. What time will y'all pick me up?"

"Well, the church is in Rosehill, and the service starts at seven. Where do you live?"

He gave directions to his sister's house, and they decided a quarter after six would be about right. Did he have a date? I mean, it was just church, and all, but still. With all that, it was hard to focus on work, resulting in mistakes when delivering those pass-outs; the toads were snarling. Along with her exasperated and annoyed looks, his boss lady aided in correcting the errors. Five o'clock would never come—until it did.

Currently without a car, he walked home, taking thirty or forty minutes to get there. As soon as he entered the door, he told Olevia about the plan for tonight. His conversation bordered on babbling. "I am meeting a new girl tonight and maybe making some new friends."

He was not hungry, and for the first time in months, he felt confident in facing the future. He couldn't explain why the excitement—it just was. His brother-in-law sat at the table and didn't exactly do handstands in celebration of his new interest in religion. But John had a job, and wasn't that the goal?

Feeling that a whole new world waited around a bend in the road that day, John showered, put on his best blue jeans and a starched white shirt, and waited. By six fifteen, he stood on the porch; at six thirty, he paced the yard. From six forty-five until seven thirty, he sat on the steps and then went into the house, disappointed.

He realized they did not have each other's phone numbers, and he didn't even know Edith's last name. She had no idea what his sister's name was. They simply had no way to contact each other.

All night, John vacillated between anger and wondering what terrible tragedy had prevented Edith from showing up. The next morning, he stood at his work post thirty minutes before clock-in time. Upon arrival, Edith ran in his direction at once.

"John, I'm so sorry. I couldn't get my car started last night and had to depend on my husband. He took us to church, but he wouldn't come to get you. I'm so sorry."

"Why wouldn't your husband pick me up?" A little doubt crept into his voice.

"Well, he doesn't like church." With tears in her eyes, she continued, "John, he's a sinner."

The sad way she said "sinner" touched John's heart. He found himself feeling sorry for the guy, as though he were the one left standing on the porch.

Edith went on to explain. "Oh, John. He'll take me and the children to church, but he won't go. I've prayed many a night for his conversion, but the Lord hasn't seen His way clear yet to give it to me. I'm sorry, John. Will you give us one more chance? Come tonight?"

"Well, I don't know. Is your car working now?"

"I think so. My boy put in a new battery last night. It got me to work this morning, but if it breaks down, I'll borrow one of the sisters' cars. I promise I'll pick you up tonight, no matter what happens."

Apology oozed from her every cell, and John still had a hankering to meet her daughter. He smiled. "I'll be on the porch at six fifteen."

At six fifteen a car, not driven by Edith, pulled up in front of the house. John leaned in and glanced at Edith through the front passenger window.

"Hey, Edith. I'm glad you made it."

"Me too. This is Ruby." She pointed at the driver. "And that's her daughter, Patty Ann, in the back."

John climbed into the back seat. By the time they got to church, he didn't care if Edith's daughter showed up or not. Patty Ann laughed at everything he said and appeared to be totally enthralled with him.

He joined in with her laughter. He could tell Edith did not share his enthusiasm, but she said nothing while they were in the car.

Once out of the car and in the churchyard, she pulled John aside. "John, Patty Ann's a nice girl, but she's a little forward. Come with me. My daughter, Ruth, is waiting at the church door."

He nodded and followed as she led the way.

There stood an angel personified: barely five feet tall, blond hair that almost reached her waist, a tiny little thing that looked as if she could sit in the palm of a human hand. Cinderella? Snow White? Rapunzel? Their images dulled when compared to Ruth's.

John's heart did an instant flip, and he stopped stone-still and stared.

Edith touched his shoulder. "Come on. Ruth's shy, so take it easy."

Without a second thought, John took step three on the way to an enlightenment he could never have imagined.

* * *

The vision of loveliness stood quietly on the church porch as Edith and John walked toward her. She dressed modestly—the very definition of chaste—and had the smile of an angel. Just thinking about it made John feel poetic! Edith brought him out of his trance.

"John, I'd like you to meet Ruth."

She held her hand out, like a princess, and he felt tempted to kiss it. That's the immediate effect this girl had on John. Holding out his hand to her felt foolish, but he didn't know what else to do.

"Hello, Ruth. My name's John. You look beautiful tonight."

She blushed and smiled. "It's nice to meet you, John."

The world stood still as John mentally counted his shortcomings, so vividly apparent in the presence of this girl. For starters, he had a pack of Camels protruding from his front shirt pocket. Instinctively, he touched it when he realized Ruth noticed them too.

"Please don't take those into church. Smoking's a sin." Ruth spoke with kindness—no condemnation, just concern.

"You know, Ruth, you're probably right about that. Let me take them back to the car."

He quickly ran back to the car, carefully placed the cigarettes where they were not likely to be crushed and dashed back to the church door.

Ruth smiled as he stood beside her and reached for her hand. They walked together up the aisle, found seats about halfway to the front and settled in together. John's nervousness prevented him from talking; he glanced at Ruth. She seemed totally at peace sitting next to him.

At six fifty-five a group of young men took the stage from a side door. Some carried tambourines, others had guitars, and one had a banjo; two kids, maybe ten or twelve years old, had spoons. While they assumed their seats, a fellow joined them onstage. He wore a fine suit (a little snug), a white shirt, a tie, and shoes that shone brightly. A mouthful of perfectly straight, white teeth and a smile that went from ear to ear softened his pudgy face. Black hair, oiled back, topped off his smooth demeanor.

In his hand, this well-dressed guy held a steel guitar that grabbed John's attention. Almost without warning, the man broke down on that instrument and started to sing with the voice of heaven. Within minutes, the audience's quiet chatter muted, and music filled every inch of the sanctuary.

"It gets sweeter, sweeter, as the days go by."

The audience tapped their feet, the tambourines kicked in and then the mandolin, the guitars, the banjo and finally the spoons. Everybody clapped their hands, and before John could take it all in, the entire congregation seemed to be singing. He looked around for a songbook, but there weren't any. People were singing the song from memory, and he sat back to enjoy the show. The fat guy slid into another song without any break in the action, and the audience followed along.

John's past church experience included a song leader who might say, "Okay, folks, let's turn to page one hundred and fifty." Not so with this group. The fat guy sang a song about testifying. He sang the first line, and the congregation responded with the next one.

"Pharaoh's got my people."

"They won't testify."

"Pharaoh's got my people."

"They won't testify."

This went on for maybe ten minutes with increasing intensity. Suddenly, a fellow jumped up to tell what God had done for him.

The more he talked, the more excited he got, and he began to do a little soft-shoe dance. He danced right out from behind the bench, into the aisle, shouting and dancing and praising the Lord. The more he danced and shouted, the louder the people clapped.

"Pharaoh's got my people," the preacher sang in a low tone.

"They won't testify," the congregation whispered their reply.

John joined in, and as the singing increased, the man's testimony grew in volume and intensity to the point that the man began to lose his breath.

Two women jumped up and did their testimony in a reciprocal fashion. One would yell and the other would shout back, while they both danced. The preacher and the congregation continued their quiet, almost whispered song.

"Pharaoh's got my people."

"They won't testify."

When John entered the church, he had expected an hour of wishing the service would be over and wanting a cigarette the entire time. Instead, he forgot about cigarettes—forgot about everything outside—and became completely absorbed by the scene going on around him. The people came across as dead serious as he observed the unique and foreign spectacle surrounding him.

The preacher eased into another song that had something to do with strange folk who practiced dancing and shouting. The gist of it was a tale about a day when people came to town and prayed the glory down.

Everybody stood up when the preacher sang, "Came to town and prayed the glory down." Song after song, testimony after testimony, John became one with the crowd. He enjoyed the show like a thirsty man after the first sip of water.

Responding to the congregation's obvious need for a break, the revival preacher walked out onstage; things quieted down a little. The congregation sat down, and the second act prepared to take the stage. The revival preacher commanded the pulpit and requested a couple of songs he liked. He pointed out a couple of different people and asked them to come down front to sing for the congregation. Every person in that room must have possessed vocal talent because no one hesitated when invited.

"Mary, you there in the second row. Give us a verse or two of that 'Great Gettin' Up Morning.' Praise Jesus. Lord. Lord."

Mary began to sing before she even left her seat. Everybody joined in with more clapping, dancing, toe tapping and testifying. John hoped he would go unnoticed, but it crossed his mind that just a pointed finger from the preacher might be enough to convince him he could sing. Such was the atmosphere they were in.

But the preacher knew the name of every person he called; as a stranger in the group, John was safe. The song service continued for about another forty-five minutes, and a designated member of the audience led every tune. Then, in unison, people sat down and became quiet while this preacher took center stage.

He preached for two hours, but John didn't complain. The guy had a way of mesmerizing his audience, making each person a part of the scene.

"You know, folks, Jesus will meet you where you are. He met Paul on the road to Damascus."

"Amen, brother," the audience responded in unison.

"He'll be there in the dark times and when the sun's shining. You know you are a sinner. He knows you are a sinner. But Jesus will meet you where you are."

"Amen, brother."

Everything the preacher said that night resonated with John. He could smell the tobacco on his clothes. He remembered the last cold beer he had. Every mistake he had ever made bubbled to the surface as he continued to listen.

Shouts of "Amen, brother" came from all sides. People jumped up, danced, kicked, and hollered. The building reverberated with sound.

"Preach on, brother, preach on."

As the service slowed to a stop, a flabbergasted John discovered he wanted it to continue. Questions filled his thoughts as they made their way to the door: *Am I really interested in the church, or is it Ruth that made it so addictive? He found it impossible to separate the two: church and Ruth. This was a new religious experience but would it have hit him so hard had he not been sitting next to Ruth?* His ability to reason faded as they walked across the parking lot. He enthusiastically took another step closer to an unfamiliar and mysterious space.

* * *

The clock struck eleven within minutes after a confused but intrigued John walked out of church that night.

He stood in the parking lot, cigarette pack heavy on his mind, but still in the car, watching the others. They lingered in clusters under the streetlights—hugging, laughing, making plans for Wednesday night. The same rituals he'd seen outside the church his mom had dragged him to occasionally. But something about tonight had been different. The way they'd sung, like they meant every word. The way the preacher had talked about God, like he was right there in the room, listening. Standing off to the side, by himself, he felt a little lost—perhaps a lot lost. Not quite outside anymore, but not inside either.

Edith left her group and appeared at his elbow, Ruth trailing behind. “Come on, John. We’ll take you home.”

The car ride passed in silence. John stared out the window at the dark streets, replaying moments from the service. The testimonial through song, he’d gripped the pew in front of him, knuckles white, feeling something pull at him he couldn’t name. He was lost in thought when the car pulled to the curb in front of Olevia’s house.

“Well, what did you think of the service?” Edith asked.

“Never seen anything like it,” John replied as he picked up his cigarettes from the floorboard. He wouldn’t light one up until he closed the front door of the house, but he surely didn’t want to forget them in the car.

“Well, I hope you’ll join us again,” Edith said as he stepped from the car.

“I might do that. Good night, Ruth.”

Once inside, John flicked his lighter and drew in that first drag. He had not changed his ways—was not even sure he wanted to—and yet, the cigarette did not taste as good as usual. Flatter. He stood at the window watching Edith’s taillights disappear, the cigarette burning between his fingers, mostly forgotten.

The next night found him sitting in a pew next to Ruth. And the night after that.

He found himself listening for Edith's car, ready before she arrived. In the services, he paid attention to the words now, not just the strangeness of it all. The preacher talked about being lost and being found about old things passing away. Was the old John passing away or was he getting lost in something he didn't yet fully understand?

On Thursday night, during the singing, John felt his throat tighten. The woman beside him had her eyes closed, one hand raised, singing about amazing grace. He didn't raise his hand. Did not close his eyes. But he felt something crack open in his chest, just a little.

By the next week, he'd stopped pretending he wasn't going. He made the revival every night that week and continued his mental battle in deciding if he was saved or not. Sure, cigarettes had lost their flavor, and when he entered a liquor store, he looked around to see who might see him paying for his beer. But he still enjoyed gulping it down. Sleep didn't provide the instant release he normally enjoyed. Instead, he found himself lost in a nighttime fog of revisiting and reconsidering everything he had heard and seen that week. Was he really different? Was he changed? No. Church was interesting, but not for him, not long-term anyway.

Sunday morning arrived with no knock on the door, no sound of Edith's struggling engine. Her car was in bad shape, and she often bummed a ride. John sat at the kitchen table with the newspaper spread in front of him, the classified section marked with circles: Cars he might afford. A Fiat that ran "more often than not"—that phrase had made him smile darkly. Wasn't that just his life? Running more often than not, sputtering along, never quite reliable. On Friday morning, he rolled into Resistol's parking lot just as Edith's husband was dropping her off for work.

"Hey, John, gotta new car?" she called as he got out.

"Yes, ma'am. And for now, it's running."

"Are you coming to church Sunday morning?"

"Planning to. Thought I might ask Ruth if I could pick her up. What do you think?"

"Sure. But you'd better call her first. Remember, she's shy."

On Sunday morning, John prayed that his car would make it to Ruth's house. He was already having alternator problems. Edith's directions were clear, but he didn't know where he was going. In fact, he wondered if he'd found the right place when he reached the end of the last dirt road. Their house looked as if it were propped up, and it certainly needed a coat of paint. The dirt yard, enclosed by a fence, revealed a couple of dogs who lay under the porch. Something about the place looked sad to John, and that surprised him.

Edith and Ruth both dressed well, not expensively but nicely, so he had figured they lived in a middle-class neighborhood; this area would be flattered by anyone who classed it lower middle class at best. He parked the Fiat and crawled out as three boys ran out the front door in his direction.

"Are you Ruth's date?" one of them yelled, giggling all the while.

"Guess so. Who are you?"

"Gerald. Ruth's my sister."

All three boys were Ruth's siblings and eager to talk. Fortunately, Edith arrived at the door and rescued him.

"Gerald, get that dog off John. Don't let him mess up his suit."

"Don't matter, ma'am. He's alright. I'm used to dogs."

Gerald dragged the mutt away while John walked up to the porch.

"Is Ruth about ready, or should I wait out here?"

"Ruth, John's here," Edith called inside and continued to talk to John.

"You have any plans for this afternoon?"

"No, ma'am."

"Well, I'm making fried chicken, if you want to come back after services."

"Sounds good."

The conversation ceased when Ruth arrived at the door looking so young and so innocent—even to nineteen-year-old John. Followed by two of her brothers, they walked toward his car until Edith called out, "Boys, you're not riding with your sister. Come on. Your daddy's taking us to church."

Despite complaining, the boys followed their mother. John opened the Fiat door, and Ruth seemed to float onto the seat. Astounded that her gracefulness made climbing into a Fiat look effortless, he closed the door and went around to the driver's side. She sat so close to the door as to be leaning on it. He wasn't surprised and chuckled as he crawled into the car.

"How old are you?"

"Fifteen."

"Is this your first date?"

"Yes."

"Well, now that you know I don't bite, it's really not necessary to polish the door handles." As usual, his attempt at humor fell flat.

"And now that you know I don't take hints, you can stop dropping them." Ruth smiled, and John's heart melted.

Little chitchat accompanied the ride to church. But Ruth radiated peace in a way that made being in her company enough.

Church came off as loud, lively, and strangely disturbing, as always. Back at her house, he enjoyed dinner and had no problem chatting with her dad, the sinner. John carefully kept enough distance so as not to look too comfortable in a sinner's circle. The day passed quickly, and the time to leave arrived way too early.

He stood up. "I guess I had better get on out of here."

"Going so soon, John? Are you coming back for service tonight?" Edith asked.

"No, ma'am. The alternator on my car's not working. Can't drive around after dark without lights." He turned to Ruth. "Walk with me out to the car?"

"I'll pick you up next Sunday morning," John said to Ruth. "Same time, okay?"

"I'll be ready."

All week long, he thought about going to church. He liked this girl, but her whole life revolved around church. He liked her church too, loved the music and even took a shine to the jumping and shouting. He enjoyed seeing it and hearing it but doubted he would ever do it.

His Sunday routine quickly became to pick up Ruth, go to church, have dinner with her family, and go home. The routine could not change much unless John got a new alternator for his car, and, within a couple of paydays, he had one.

On the way to Sunday service, he mentioned it to Ruth. "Guess what? Nighttime visits might be available to us! I got a new alternator on the car."

"Oh, I'm so glad. There's a powerful preacher supposed to come over to Davis Street Auditorium. I want to hear him. Would you?"

"Sure. Can't wait! What night?" To soften the annoyance in his tone, he added a smile.

Her response sounded serious. "John, when are you going to get saved?"

"I think I'm pretty close now. I'm not smoking, hardly ever have a beer, and you're the only girl I'm seeing."

"That's not the same! You must get saved, sanctified, and filled with a separate in-filling of the Holy Ghost with evidence of speaking in unknown tongues."

She said all of that in just one breath. She sounded so much like an Edith recording that John's head almost did one of those exorcist spins. *Geez. I am not even sure what she said. Maybe I oughta get out of here right now.* That thought quickly evaporated to make room for: *I like this girl, and I think I can get around this religion thing. At least, I'm gonna try.*

"I might do all that stuff someday, but for now, I'm just not smoking." His joke had an audience of one: himself. Ruth continued her spiel as if he had not spoken. For a minute he wondered if Ruth had seen through him. Of course, he was still smoking but convinced himself he wasn't lying to Ruth because he never, ever smoked in her presence.

Ruth continued, "The preacher's name is Gene Ewing. Let's go Friday night. It starts at seven."

No use fighting the inevitable. "Okay. I'll pick you up at six, and we'll get a hot dog on the way."

And without any fight, John leaned into step five, about to see the glimmer of the road ahead.

* * *

Friday, John pulled out his wallet to pay for the gas and stared at the cigarettes behind the counter. He had agreed that smoking was sinful, but how bad could it be? He had told Ruth he wasn't smoking, but surely, she heard the implied "for now" part. It would be okay to have one every now and again. He decided to always answer her smoking inquiries with "I'm not smoking for now." He pulled out an extra dollar and slipped the cigarettes into his pocket.

That night he got cleaned up for his Dairy Queen date before the revival and left the house feeling in control of everything. After their dinner and just before leaving the Dairy Queen, he saw the cigarettes were still in his pocket instead of safely stored under the car seat. Quickly excusing himself, he rushed to the bathroom, slid the half-empty pack down his sock, and walked confidently back to join Ruth.

"Are you about ready? It's six thirty, and we'll want to get a good seat."

"I am. John, I'm so excited to see Reverend Ewing and having you next to me makes it even more special."

John muttered, "Me, too."

They walked out to the car, and by six forty-five, entered the Davis Street Auditorium, ready to see and hear what Ruth referred to as this renowned man of God, Gene Ewing.

About fifteen hundred, maybe two thousand, people were already in the arena. The hushed voices created a buzz. The air of expectancy filled John's nostrils like the smell of popcorn and cotton candy in a circus tent. A band on stage set about getting their performance structure perfected. Three members picked a little bluegrass, while others played something that sounded like the blues. The remaining members tuned their instruments.

John and Ruth found a couple of seats just as a lead man bounced onto the stage. He welcomed everyone, and John felt the two of them shared a meeting of the souls when their eyes momentarily locked. Though the request to prepare for an anointing focused on the crowd, John felt singled out. The man eased into his love of music and music's ability to calm the roaring beast and stop the devil in his tracks.

On cue, the bluegrass band—a fiddle player, two banjos, a steel guitar, and a mandolin—struck up a tune. Sometimes one of the musicians would sing a couple of verses in that high, long, lonesome sound so associated with bluegrass.

With an ease grown of hours of practice, the bluegrass slid into ordinary country gospel, and the congregation swayed, hummed, clapped quietly, and sang in hushed tones. Seemingly without effort, the band morphed into what John assumed was Christian rock, and the music shook the walls. People sang, many shouted amen, and other attendees called hallelujah. No sad faces marred the scene or damaged the growing euphoria.

About forty-five minutes into the hypnotic musical festival, Brother Gene Ewing materialized from behind the curtains; as if a switch were flipped, a hush fell over the crowd. He ambled to center stage and stood silent for a minute or more as he surveyed his audience. As people began to fidget, his booming voice attracted everyone's attention to him.

"Let's pray. God, we're here tonight for an anointing. Convict us of our devil ways. Lord, make us open vessels to be filled with your Holy Spirit. Break our hearts so we can hear the word of God. Amen."

To John, the words sounded a bit harsh for a church service, but he had promised Ruth *no snap judgments*. Everyone stood. Surprisingly, he did too. He quickly sat down, as did the others around him.

Brother Ewing began by talking about and reading parts of the Sermon on the Mount. Now this was more comfortable, comparable with the Baptist sermons of his youth. His mind settled into a quiet place, remembering yesteryears made better by the music intro.

Suddenly, Brother Ewing slapped his Bible down on the podium, and everyone sat up straighter.

"People, my people, God's people, if you have your Bibles, turn to Malachi 3:7–12."

He allowed a little time for those who wished to, to find the scripture. A sudden shout caused everyone, especially John, to visibly jump.

"Will a man rob God? Will a *man* rob God?"

Hallelujahs escaped from the listeners, and the organist played "Who's on the Lord's Side."

That served as the cue for about ten men carrying baskets to stand, before wandering among the pews full of people. A couple of the men silently shook their heads and said, "Will a *man* rob God?"

He made sure he threw in a couple of dollars. The band's rendition of "There's Power in the Blood" replaced the quieter organ music.

The baskets were emptied and refilled more than once.

Brother Ewing took a moment to regain his composure. On the side stage, he mopped his brow, took deep breaths, and in a barely audible voice said, "Thank you, Lord."

Immediately, the band went into their final song, "What Hast Thou Done for Me." About the middle of the first verse, Brother Ewing returned to center stage, and the men with baskets sat down.

"Ladies and gentlemen, tonight I'm gonna tell you about the devils in this room!" he yelled and shook his fist. "The devils are combing this room. They're after my people, God's people." He slammed his fist on the podium.

"Get thee behind me, Satan!" he shouted. "There's somebody in this room who suffers from stomach trouble."

He rubbed his hands on his forehead. "It's cancer. Lord, describe this man to me. I see him. I see him. Thank you, Lord."

Out of nowhere, a fellow came running up one of the aisles. Brother Ewing touched him, and on the spot, the afflicted man fell backward. He looked visibly weak and must have fainted. A couple of men came from behind the curtain to throw a sheet over him.

What was going on? Was the man okay? None of the congregation appeared troubled. The congregation sat and stared at the sheet-covered man. Within seconds, the man rose up, still under the sheet. He cried and talked in a language Ruth explained to be "tongues." To John, it sounded like gibberish. Eventually, the man sat in one of the pews, rubbing his head and shouting hallelujah every so often.

Brother Ewing explained, "Jesus met this man in his cancer-infected state, and He healed him. Not me. No. Jesus healed him. I'm only an instrument. Praise the Lord. How are you feeling tonight?"

Physically impaired people from the audience began to line up. John had not seen these people when he and Ruth arrived. Had they all sat together, or were they kept in a separate room? Brother Ewing broke into his contemplation when he spoke directly to disabled people and the infirm coming toward the podium.

"Brothers and sisters! Don't climb those stairs. Jesus will meet you where you are. I'm coming to you." With that, he left the stage and reappeared standing in front of it.

John hadn't seen any of these disabled people when he walked into the church. Surely in an audience of likely over two thousand people, he could not have seen everybody. The devil must be at work in his mind, leading him to doubt; he had to fight him off.

Brother Ewing continued to preach and to touch people, causing them to fall to the floor—and a number of them also spoke in tongues. He even took crutches from crippled people and threw those crutches away. Every time, the person appeared to be completely healed as they danced down the aisles.

The most dramatic healing event involved a woman sitting in a wheelchair, clearly crying as she tried to push her chair forward.

"Stay there, sister, I'm coming to you. Jesus is coming to you." Brother Ewing almost ran toward her.

"Sister, how long have you suffered the atrocity of sitting in a wheelchair, unable to walk?"

"Since my surgery, three years ago," she sobbed. "I want to walk again. Please, Jesus."

"Jesus is here. He hears your plea, and He's ready to meet you where you are. Do you have faith for it? Do you believe Jesus can heal you?"

"I do." She continued to sob.

Brother Ewing touched the woman on her forehead while he touched his own. "Jesus says, 'Get up and walk.'" With that, he jerked her out of the chair and kicked it ten feet away. John expected her to fall to the floor, but she danced and shouted back to a seat in the audience.

People were *cured* of all sorts of diseases, including a smattering of illnesses they didn't even know they had. Lost in this twilight zone and caught up in everything happening around him, he focused on Brother Ewing, who appeared to turn in his direction at exactly that moment.

"There's somebody in this room who has the nicotine devil. Is it you? Are you fighting alone? Jesus will meet you where you are."

John at once believed Brother Ewing had been led by Jesus to contact him. If nicotine was a devil, John had it. Rather, it had John. Suddenly, he smelled it on his clothes. Generally, he liked the smell, but not tonight, not surrounded by these folks.

Out of the corner of my eye, he saw the basket men wandering again through the crowd.

Brother Ewing took control of the crowd again. "God is speaking to me. God will deliver His people, my people, from the nicotine devil."

He paused for emphasis and to allow the basket men to set up in pivotable places around the auditorium. Then he continued, "God has spoken to me. God says, 'Trust Me.' Show God you trust Him. Show Him *TONIGHT* that you believe His Holy Word. Throw your cigarettes into God's baskets. God is waiting for you to trust Him. Can He trust you?"

You could hear the rustle all over the arena as people dug out their cigarettes. John reached into his sock and retrieved his almost half pack of Camels. Without another thought, he stood and threw them into the nearest basket; he heard people around him shout, "Amen, brother."

He had forgotten Ruth still sat beside him. As he sat down, their eyes met. She looked so hurt, so disappointed, that he instantly felt guilty.

"You told me you had quit."

"I had cut down a lot. They're gone now."

Her radiant smile told him she held no anger or condemnation. All was well.

For three hours, Brother Ewing continued to share God's plan for every life. Multiple people who had thrown their cigarettes into the baskets now ran down the aisles. Brother Ewing ran from the front of the arena to meet them halfway. The ones he touched fell to the floor, kicked, shouted, and spewed forth more of the unknown tongues.

Every time it happened, the preacher got more excited, and the more excited he was, the more uncontrolled the audience became. John wondered if a riot might break out right there, but things eventually came to a natural ending, and everyone found their way out of the building.

Ruth and John left, and he dropped her off at home; then he stopped by Mr. M's and bought a pack of Camels.

* * *

When John got ready for work the next morning, he felt uneasy, as if something bad might happen.

He continued to hear in his mind the preacher say, *Can He trust you?* He smoked more the night before and that morning than he typically did in a week. In fact, he picked up another pack on the way to work, and every time he inhaled, mentally he heard, *Can He trust you?*

That nicotine devil had a hold on him, like a rat caught in a trap.

He began to picture nicotine devils in his mind every time he flipped his Zippo lighter, but he kept right on sucking those cigarettes nonstop. By the time he reached the time clock, he knew the nicotine devil had robbed him of Ruth. She wouldn't want him anymore because he had lied to her. He was possessed by something stronger than her and stronger than himself. She knew God couldn't trust him.

He waved to Edith and went over to stand at his post, and Edith walked over.

"Well, John, Ruth said y'all enjoyed the service last night." She smiled.

"Brother Gene Ewing was powerfully good—an experience I'll never forget."

She glanced at his shirt. "Wonder why you still have those cigarettes in your pocket?"

"No reason to deny it. The nicotine devil has me in his clutches. I threw 'em away last night after Brother Ewing said God would deliver me. Then I bought more on the way home."

Again, she just smiled, no redress. "Ruth sent you a letter."

She reached for her purse and took out a folded note, and the whistle blew. Time to go to work.

John put the note in his pocket, right next to his cigarettes and the nicotine devil. The morning dragged on until lunchtime finally arrived. He ran to the parking lot, lit up a cigarette, and read that two-and-a-half-page letter.

Ruth told him of her all-night prayers and that Jesus had spoken to her. She wanted him to know that Jesus could do anything but lie, and He would free John from the nicotine devil. Jesus loved him and would meet him where he was. The letter went on to explain that Jesus made those promises to her last night as she prayed.

She closed the letter by declaring that she thought she was in love with John and would spend the entire day praying for him.

As he refolded the letter and returned it to his pocket, he thought, *Lordy, what in the world has Jesus done now!* Most of the time, he thought he was doing a little play-acting, but sometimes he thought he wasn't. Now Ruth had talked to Jesus about him, eliciting all sorts of promises.

He smiled to himself as he considered the situation: *Well, Jesus has his work cut out for him.* But he felt sure there would be no shouting or dancing or speaking in gibberish in his future.

He finished his cigarette, ground it out under his foot on the pavement and went back to work.

He felt as nervous as a long-tailed cat in a room full of rocking chairs. Every time he cupped his hand to light a cigarette, he'd glance in Edith's direction. If she happened to look at him, he became physically ill; he had indigestion, his throat burned, and the cigarette didn't sit right. In his agitated state, he gave too many pass-out hats to the wrong woman.

The toad next to her screamed, "Look at whatcha' doing! I ain't got no number eighty-nines yet, and you done gave her two racks."

He apologized and tried to concentrate on his job. When he wasn't smoking, he clicked his Zippo open and shut. Before long, those clicks began to sound like *Can He trust you?*

When five o'clock came, he was in a bad way and hurried to his car.

Edith called across the lot, "Wait up, John!"

He stopped in his tracks, facing his car and taking deep breaths to calm the nausea. Edith took a deep breath or two of her own, from scurrying across the parking lot.

Gasping for air, she said, "Don't forget we're praying for you. I talked to a couple of the sisters, and they agree God is going to deliver you from the nicotine devil. God can't lie." She patted him on the shoulder as he nodded and got into his car.

When he arrived at Olevia's house, nobody was home, which made it a little easier to go inside. Sweat rolled from his brow, and he shook as if he were having a chill. Good thoughts came, quickly replaced by scary ones. Thinking he could get his mind straight, he went to the Jupiter Lanes bowling alley, took a seat at the snack bar and ordered a Coke. He tried talking to a young waitress, whom he knew well, but the conversation proved stilted, uncomfortable for both. In half an hour, he parked in front of Olevia's duplex again.

Sleep was elusive that night and for multiple nights afterwards. He wavered between believing the nicotine devil was at work and fearing he might have a nervous breakdown. Sleep-deprived and nauseous, he made it through the week. Come Sunday morning, his Fiat skidded and squished up Ruth's long, muddy driveway. All the while, he knew something important lay ahead.

Ruth's brothers ran out when they got a glimpse of the Fiat. They behaved as if John carried the title of Smartest Guy in the World. Seeing them headed in his direction cheered him. He stopped to visit with them and played with the dog until Ruth came out.

"Good morning, John," she called as she stepped off the porch.

He looked up at the angelic vision. "Hey, you ready? You look beautiful this morning."

"Yes, I'm ready," she said as she got into the car.

John sensed a chasm between them. It was deserved. After all, as a sinner with so many devils, what else could he expect from a girl who looked like the pure-of-heart personified? He closed her door, then his, and they drove to church. The heavy silence punctuating the air made him look forward even more to finding his place in a pew.

The quiet atmosphere between them continued once they were inside the church. Soon, the church leaders fired up their regular song service, and a welcome sense of peace flowed over him. The band played and the people sang—all the regulars, as well as a couple he had not heard before. Then came the real surprise.

Brother Maxfield, that Sunday's preacher, walked onstage from a side door. By the time he reached the pulpit, the crowd had quieted. Following his usual lengthy pause while he scanned the congregation, his eyes locked on Edith.

"Sister Edith, do you reckon we could get you and Sister Ruth to sing a special song for us this morning?"

To John's amazement, they didn't even hesitate. They just stood up as one, laid down their purses and walked to the front. He stared, wondering what would come next.

Edith said something to the guitar player, who responded, "Just start it. I'll find it."

When the song started, it was obvious he did not have to look hard to find it. The song was called "Heaven," and John memorized the chorus. He had time to do so because they sang every verse to the congregation's shouts of "Amen!" "Sing it, sisters!" and "Lord, I'm coming home!"

Heaven supernal (happy home above)
Heaven supernal (land of peace and love)
(Oh, it makes me feel like traveling on)
Heaven supernal, Heaven eternal
(I'm so glad it's real)[1]

---

1 Written by Boyd and Helen McSpadden first released in 1960.

Edith sang "Heaven," and Ruth answered with "supernal." They harmonized with each response. John believed it to be the most beautiful sound he'd ever heard, and when they walked back to the pew, he swelled with pride, as if he had done the singing.

A dozen people or more walked, one by one, to the front of the church to testify, but eventually, interest in the service dwindled. Suddenly, Brother Drawhorn, a regular in church most Sundays, jumped up, and John almost did the same. Brother Drawhorn, seated directly behind John, hollered. John turned to get a better view of the commotion and to hear these words: "I won't take it no more, you dirty, low-down devil, you." Drawhorn looked as if he were wrestling with an imaginary person and had that person in a headlock. Without warning, it appeared the invisible foe got the best of him. He hit the bench, rolled onto the floor, and slid into the aisle.

People shouted, "Hallelujah, brother, hallelujah! Fight that devil!"

Brother Drawhorn fought up and down the center aisle, at times almost reaching the door, only to be dragged back in. He yelled and stomped.

The crowd continued to shout encouragement. "Jesus is with you! Fight that devil! Hallelujah! Praise the Lord."

After probably ten minutes, he reached the door and held his hand up as if he were holding something by the collar. He knocked the door open and kicked his leg high in the air.

"Now, you get out of here, you low-down, dirty devil. Don't you ever come back. This is God's house."

He turned to the congregation, looking worn out, but pleased. He hollered one more time, "Hallelujah! Praise Jesus, Hallelujah!"

The shouting, clapping, singing, and testifying seemed to rock the building. Pandemonium took over the auditorium. John had never seen anything like it, and he worried a bit about Drawhorn's health, as he was a chubby man about fifty years old.

No one else seemed concerned as the preacher sang, "I am a happy, happy millionaire. My father's rich, and I am his only heir."

The crowd soon quieted a bit and joined in with the song, and that's when John lost control of his mind and his body. He saw and experienced every bad thing he had ever done in his entire life. He heard every bad word he had ever said, and he remembered every unclean thought that had crossed his mind.

He didn't want any more cigarettes, not another bottle of beer. His only desire was to get acquainted with Jesus. He could feel Him, as real as anything that had ever happened in his life. Tears ran down his face, and he knew he shouted gibberish.

In his next memory, he opened his eyes to see church sisters standing over him. They were fanning him, smiling, and shouting, "Praise the Lord!" His eyes searched for Ruth, and at that moment, she touched his face.

"Hallelujah! Jesus answered my prayers just like He said He would. Praise Jesus, John. You are saved. Praise Jesus."

The preacher came over next as the sisters helped him to his feet.

"Brother John, you've had an experience this morning. Will you come back and tell us about it tonight?"

"Amen, brother. I'll be here."

He would say later, "As God is my witness, I don't remember anything more about that experience than what's written above."

* * *

All Sunday afternoon, he thought of nothing except that life-changing experience. He and Ruth drove home, and he stayed all afternoon, pacing the floor and talking about what he had to share with people. Ruth's dad, the sinner, became the first victim.

"Earl, I want to talk to you about Jesus."

"John, I *live* with Edith and Ruth. Do you think I haven't *heard* about Jesus?"

"I know, I know. I was just like you, but now I know Jesus . . . "

Earl took his chair and went outside to sit. Before John could follow him, Ruth touched his shoulder.

"John, no use talking to Daddy. We can pray for him."

John nodded, and they did just that, right there on the spot. Edith joined in, and the little boys looked amused. Pretty soon, they went outside but John couldn't really calm down.

The food tasted better, the sun shone brighter, and he felt driven to tell people, to share the gospel.

He got his chance at the evening service.

He and Ruth took seats near the front of the chapel and talked quietly while they waited for *showtime*.

John scrutinized every detail involved in the pre-show setup, from when the band members first came out to the congregation's response to the ballooning excitement. He could smell the change in the atmosphere as the musicians played warm-up tunes.

He absorbed the most minute particulars of the song service as it groomed the crowd for Brother Maxfield to take center stage. Once he walked out, it felt like the audience was palpably handed over to him, as if he had reached for the reins of a stubborn horse.

"Praise Jesus. It's good to see every one of you in God's house tonight. Hallelujah."

"Praise Jesus. Amen," the worshippers answered.

"Tonight, we have a special treat in store for us. Brother John—Brother John, would you stand up? Brother John met Jesus this morning, right here, right in this room. Lord, Lord, it was a powerful meeting. Praise Jesus!"

"Amen, brother." The response felt programmed, as if a "Praise Jesus" or a "Hallelujah" required an "Amen."

"Well, tonight, good people, Brother John's going to share his testimony. He's going to tell us what it's like to meet Jesus in the depths of sin and be washed as clean as the driven snow. Praise Jesus!"

"Amen. Hallelujah. Jesus, speak to me."

By now, John squirmed in his pew, not because of nerves but rather because he had a driving need to share the Good News. He wanted every person in that auditorium to know Jesus stood ready, willing, and able to save them from an eternity in hell.

He realized he had watched other people with a jaundiced eye as they spouted their religious experiences. He didn't understand and could not fully explain what had happened to him, but he felt compelled to tell everybody how his experience transformed him. So, before Brother Maxfield had time to invite him to the podium, he bounded up onto the stage.

"Brother Maxfield, I don't just *want to* tell these people what happened to me. I *have to* tell them. The Holy Ghost grabbed me this morning and shook the devil out. Praise Jesus!"

"Amen, brother."

Brother Maxfield took a seat next to the deacons, effectively handing his crowd to John, who couldn't stop talking. He had a lot to say, and the more he said, the more excited he got. The more into it he got, the more the people joined in, creating an emotional frenzy.

They shook that building.

He testified for a while. Then somebody jumped out of their seat and gave their own testimony. At any lull, John took over again, testifying and thanking Jesus for saving his soul from eternal fire. The band chimed in with loud soft-rock gospel tunes, as if it had been planned that way. And maybe it had been?

When they played "Millionaire," John gave the grateful congregation an opportunity to share their material wealth with God. John doubted anyone in the congregation knew he could talk that much. The more he talked, the more excited he got, exactly like those other men he had seen. At once, he knew he had gotten religion, as he had heard it explained so many times. He knew he must preach and tell everyone who would listen about this wonderful experience.

Immediately following that morning's conversion, he began to study his Bible. He embarked on a love affair with Jesus, and that night he felt the need to share what he felt. The ten men who normally passed receptacles among the people appeared from somewhere with collection plates in hand. In the aisles, Brother Maxfield met with the lucky sanctified congregants filled with the Holy Spirit.

After a wild evening, John walked into his bedroom at eleven o'clock. Though exhausted, he was too exhilarated to sleep as he mentally reviewed every nuance of his experience. He vowed to read nothing except the Bible. If he listened to the radio, it would be KSKY, the religious station.

The next Sunday, one of the deacons asked him to teach a Sunday School class—the Juniors, eleven- and twelve-year-olds. He gratefully agreed. His world focused on bringing lost souls to Jesus. After a Sunday morning church service, he often got together a half-dozen brothers to accompany him to a downtown Garland street corner.

They brought their guitars and found a merchant who would allow the amplifiers to be plugged in. The guys played, and John preached. He wanted every person to know Jesus and found it difficult to understand why so many people would not listen. Brother Maxfield asked him to hold a couple of revival meetings there at the church.

He looked in the mirror and said aloud, "Lord, I am becoming a man of God! Praise Jesus."

He then sat down and wrote a letter to his dad.

Dear Daddy,

I've been saved. Jesus is my Master now. The nicotine devils and alcohol devils don't control me anymore. I'm preaching the Word of God. I love you, Daddy, and Jesus does too.

Your son,
John

Within a week, he received a reply.

Dear John,

I always told you about that stuff. I hate it happened where it did, but I'm glad that is where you are. Ain't none of it bad.

Love,
Dad

John kept on keeping on. He loved preaching. He loved praying. Just reading the Bible did not satisfy him; he had to *study* what he read. Perhaps it was the studying that produced the fly in the buttermilk. Well, that plus more good nights' sleep.

"Study to show thyself worthy."

The apostle Paul said that, and good advice it is. At least, that's what John thought, but the more he studied, the cloudier the issues became.

When he approached his Bible reading with attention only to the surface words, everything was fine. He preached those lessons, said "Praise Jesus," and the crowds answered "Amen." Everybody was happy.

But, as soon as he scoured the scriptures for deeper meanings, alarm bells went off in his mind. He decided he must be alone too much to see things clearly.

"Ruth, I'm lonely. I know you won't be sixteen until next month, but I think we both know our hearts. I know Jesus knows our hearts."

"I know mine, John. I want to spend the rest of my life with you. Besides, I prayed to marry a preacher. Jesus answered my prayer." She smiled, and his heart melted.

Much had happened to him during the year that he looked at Fort Polk through a rearview mirror: three or four jobs, being saved by the blood of Jesus and slain in the spirit, and now he could be the answer to somebody's prayer! Wow!

That very night, he and Ruth talked to Edith and Earl. Until then, he did not know that Earl was Ruth's stepfather, but it made no difference. Everybody, including her biological dad, provided Amens to their decision.

Of course, there were still a couple of hurdles to jump.

The Texas age of consent law frowned on marriages between couples of their ages.

"I'll sign for Ruth," Edith suggested.

"Well, I can tell you, right off, my daddy won't sign anything like that for me. He don't do such as that."

Edith had the answer. She grinned and exclaimed, "Mississippi. That's where we need to go so you two can get hitched. I'll go with you to sign for Ruth, and the age of majority there is eighteen for men. No use in anybody having to lie about ages."

"I'm afraid my car won't make it to Mississippi."

Earl spoke up. "You can use my car if you can be back in less than a week. Take Edith with you."

"That sounds good, but I don't have the money to do that."

Edith offered the financial solution. "One hundred dollars would do it. Let's go over to First National of Garland. I know a guy there named Meazel. He'll okay a personal note if I vouch for you."

John's mind raced. Ruth would be sixteen in days. "Okay. If I can get that cash on July fifth, we'll go to Mississippi on July sixth. How's that for a birthday present, Ruth?"

She blushed and smiled while her parents nodded their approval. John beamed and thought, *Boy, does life get any better than this?*

The sun had yet to peek over the horizon when Edith, Ruth and John backed Earl's green 1962 Chevy out of the garage. Heading to Mississippi with the A/C humming on high, the skies clear and the love of his life sitting next to him, John knew paradise awaited around the corner.

* * *

They rolled into Woodville, Mississippi, as the clock struck nine that morning. Woodville looked like as good a place as any town to begin a dream or end a nightmare. He parked in front of the courthouse, and the three of them strode in. Three women stood behind the counter.

Three women! Why would Woodville, Mississippi, need three women working at the courthouse? Surely, there's not that much municipal activity going on in Woodville. Guess that's a government job perk. Why that thought caused him to smile, he did not know. But he appreciated the opportunity to smile.

He walked up to the clerk. "Ma'am. We're here to get married. Can you help us?"

"Sure. Take a seat on the bench there, and I'll call one of our justices of the peace."

They sat for a thirty-minute eternity.

Finally, a middle-aged man, probably six feet tall, ambled through the door. He wore overalls, knee-high black rubber boots and a long-sleeved white shirt that seemed out of place. He was barrel-chested and slightly winded. His sun-worn face confessed to years of manual labor. He walked slowly to the counter, all the while mopping his brow with a red handkerchief.

It was July, and he appeared to have left in the middle of a job. At the counter, he and one of the women conversed for a minute or two before she pointed in the direction of the three of them. He motioned them to follow him into a small office to the right of the counter. He closed the door behind them.

"So, y'all want to get married?" He fell more than sat in the chair behind the desk.

"Yes, sir."

"How old are you, son?"

"Nineteen. Be twenty next month."

"And you?" He looked at Ruth. "How old?"

"Sixteen, sir. Today."

He then turned to Edith. "What part do you play in all this?"

"I'm her mother."

"Okay. She'll need a permission slip signed. You can take care of that."

John thought, *Permission slip? Sounds like she's going on a school field trip!* It certainly made her sound young, and just for a moment, a cold chill ran up his back. One look at Ruth, and he shook it off.

"Son, I'll need your driver's license. Prove your age and get an address. Once you're married, I'll mail a letter to that address. Three days are permitted to get this union annulled. If it's not, then this here is a legal marriage."

That didn't concern John. The Garland address on his license belonged to his sister, and she was in Maine. No one would complain or dispute the wedding. John handed over his driver's license, and the justice of the peace copied the necessary information before returning it. Shoving the papers to the side, he stood up.

"Okay. Do you have a ring?"

"No, sir."

"Fine. I'll skip that part. . . . "

Things moved quickly, and in less than ten minutes, they were married; it didn't really feel real.

"What do I owe you, sir?"

"Ya got two dollars?"

"Yes, sir."

"Give it to me, and we're square. Congratulations, and good luck to you both."

John handed over the two dollars as the justice of the peace gathered his papers and left.

John should have been a happy fellow, and he was and he wasn't. "I pronounce you man and wife" sounded more like a verdict with a long prison sentence attached than the key to paradise. Edith appeared more elated than either Ruth or John. Certainly, they wanted to be married, but lifetime commitments at their age? Besides, they knew little about each other outside of church and reading the Bible. John was eerily aware that he may have vowed to be someone he was unprepared to be.

"Well, you're all grown up now, Ruth. You got yourself a husband and a good one, I think."

Ruth's sad expression spoke volumes, one of which gave John a brief glimpse: Maybe Edith made the decision more than Ruth. He simply stared at her until she met his eyes and smiled. At least, whatever the future brings, they were in this together. They both relaxed a bit.

"If y'all don't mind, I'm not really ready to go back to Texas yet. I'd like to stop by Tioga to see my daddy. It only takes a couple of hours to get there. What do you think?" Perhaps looking at the home where he grew up and standing in front of his dad as a grown man, with a wife, would be enough to clear his concerns completely.

Neither Edith nor Ruth objected. John's dad worked on the switch engine that ran right in front of his house. It so happened that they arrived at the railroad crossing as the train approached. John slowed and waved, and his dad recognized him. He stopped the engine right there and leaned out.

"What are you doing here?"

"Daddy, I just got married."

"Married?"

"Yes, sir. I've got my wife and mother-in-law with me."

His Dad said something to his fireman, and then he climbed down from the engine. As he walked over to the car, his eyes lit up at the sight of Edith. He had another smile for John, who remembered his dad had always had an eye for the ladies.

"Where are you going to stay tonight?" he asked before John introduced Ruth or Edith.

"We're stopping by Mrs. Curry's. I guess we'll stay there," John answered.

"Oh, no. I live in an empty house." He laughed. "I need company. Why don't y'all go on up there and make yourselves at home? I'll be there about five or so."

"Okay, if that's okay with you."

"Sure. Now, introduce me to your new relatives."

All three of them climbed out of the car for John to make the introductions. His dad smiled, hugged John, hugged them, shook hands, and personified southern hospitality. Emotional outbursts—at least the kind that involved hugging—where John was involved were a rarity in John's memory. It felt strange, and after a couple of minutes of chitchat, his dad scrambled up the ladder and into the cab of the railroad engine.

John, Ruth, and Edith turned into Mrs. Curry's driveway. Another round of introductions and hugs occurred. They had coffee, Mrs. Curry brought out a blackberry cobbler and whipped cream, and John relished the olfactory delight, reminding him of old times with Mrs. Curry. They all enjoyed a good visit before heading up the hill to his dad's house. Things began to look up.

Once there, they settled into rocking chairs on the front porch to wait for his daddy. Sure enough, at five o'clock his dad's black Chevy truck roared up the driveway, throwing up rocks and dust all the way. He hopped out, all smiles and welcoming gestures.

"I'm glad y'all are here. I don't do much cooking, but—"

Edith interrupted, "Mr. Yeager, I would be honored to cook us a meal. Just show me where you keep everything."

"Well, now, it does feel good to come home to a woman in the kitchen," he replied with a wink.

John smiled. Ruth stared, and his dad and Edith seemed to have their own private joke going on. They both giggled like teenagers or something. She followed him into the kitchen while Ruth and John stood around, not exactly sure what their next move should be. A stranger would have assumed they barely knew each other, while his dad and Edith were old friends, laughing and banging pots and pans in the kitchen.

As if a bell rang, they turned toward either other simultaneously and chuckled before moving into the living room to wait for dinner. John couldn't tell if his dad liked his new wife but had no doubt he was clearly taken with his mother-in-law. As they sat in rocking chairs and chatted, Ruth commented with a smile, "Well, I think our parents are going to get along."

John responded, "That's a start." And the mood continued to lighten. All four of them had an enjoyable evening.

The next morning, Ruth and John shared a devotional. Only the two of them attended because his dad and Edith had gone shopping. He bought Edith a case of nylon hose, the only purchase made that day. John wondered how many pairs of hose came in a case, and his dad explained by saying that, as a church-going woman, Edith needed plenty of stockings. They laughed and teased each other nonstop until John realized it was time to get on the road. His dad got a bit serious as they were walking out to the car; he called Ruth and John to the side.

"Ya'll are too young, and you don't know what you've done. But you've already done it. So, I hope the best for you."

They both stared as if they couldn't decide if they had been chastised or congratulated or both. He gave each of them twenty dollars, said it was gas money, turned and walked into the house. He returned to his own world and left them to theirs.

On the plus side, John loved Ruth, and he was determined to do his best to be a good Christian husband—if only he could figure out what that was! He knew instinctively that Ruth felt the same way about her role as a wife.

There might be bumps in the road, but he knew their love would carry them through. He reached for Ruth's hand as she got into the car.

"I love you." He smiled as he spoke.

Ruth returned his affection with a brief kiss and a hug. "I love you too, John."

The sun shone brighter, and all doubts disappeared.

* * *

They set up housekeeping in a square building consisting of one bedroom, one bath, a kitchen, and a living room.

Twenty dollars of his dad's forty-dollar donation paid the first month's rent, and TG&Y got the majority of the other twenty in exchange for two plates, two forks, two spoons, two cups, two glasses, a pot and frying pan. John even had a couple of bucks left over.

Edith's husband, the sinner, brought over a single bed, and Edith gave them sheets. The first steps of their journey together began. John preached as often as he was asked and sometimes when he wasn't.

Every church he visited provided a love offering for his services, and, although there wasn't enough love in those baskets to support them, it helped to smooth the rough places. He still manned his Resistol post, but his heart leaned toward spreading the Word and saving souls.

Almost every minute he wasn't working at Resistol or preaching, he studied the Bible, continuing to grow in understanding of the Scripture as it should be lived. Ruth read it while John was at work, and at night, they pored over the scriptures together. In the absence of a radio, a television or the money for a movie, the Bible provided their free-time activity. They read aloud to each other, discussed every word, and assumed the roles of the characters in their quest for greater spiritual understanding. Together, they overcame their initial fear of going below those surface words to find enhanced lessons and wisdom.

John carried his Bible everywhere he went. One hot night, he and Ruth drove to White Rock Lake to enjoy a breath of fresh air. With the windows down and the car parked in the shade near a streetlamp, they began their meditation ritual.

After dark, the low light required that they lean in close to see the text. Once they read something, they sat up to discuss it. This up and down activity went on for a length of time before a policeman pulled in behind them, lights flashing. He sidled up to John's window.

"What are you two doing, buddy?"

"Reading the Bible."

"Smart alecks don't fare well with me. Step out of the car."

John stepped out, holding his Bible in one hand and extending the other to shake the policeman's hand.

"I'm Brother John Yeager, and this is my wife, Ruth. Sir, we didn't mean to upset you none. The breeze on the lake is nicer out here, cooler than it is at home. The light's not too good, but we manage. Is there a law against reading the Bible in this park?"

The cop appeared to be in a trance, as if hypnotized, not believing his ears or his eyes. He did not shake John's hand, just stood there staring. John conceded later that old Lucifer made him enjoy the moment so much. To break the silence, John spoke again.

"Sir, have you met Jesus? I'd like to tell you about him. Me and my wife, we've got a love affair going with Jesus."

With no hint of humor, the officer recovered from his surprise. "Look, this is no place for you two to park."

"Not even to read our Bible?" John asked incredulously.

"Not to do anything. You better move on along now."

John sized him up a little, put on his best *I-pity-you, a-poor-sinner* look and took one more jab.

"I understand that, Officer. The devil's hands have covered your eyes and bound your soul. You know, Jesus loves you, and he wants to loosen those ropes from around your heart. Can we have a word of prayer together, brother?"

The cop began to loosen up, and John thought he saw a slight grin—maybe it was a smirk—cross his face.

"The only word we're sharing is goodbye, my friend."

He turned and headed back to his car. Ruth and John drove home with a story to share—which they did, both among friends and multiple times in John's sermons. That officer had no idea how many people in Garland prayed for him!

Months passed, and the days seemed to melt into each other. John appeared happy on the surface, but something gnawed at his mind. Just as he first met Jesus in one church service, he re-met himself in another.

John's church friends had visited another church—one pastored by a woman, no less. John was a bit skeptical of Sister Casey because he hadn't yet made a complete decision about the Bible's teaching regarding a woman's place in the church, or anywhere else, for that matter.

On a Sunday night, one of Ruth's friends told them she had been to Sister Casey's church that morning.

"Brother John, I told Sister Casey about you."

"What about me?"

"Well, just that you were a new preacher, and God was working miracles through you. She said she would like to meet you and asked me to encourage you and Ruth to visit her congregation."

"I don't know if that's a good idea." Why would he want to visit another church when their current church provided the gospel?

Ruth joined in, "I bet she would call you to the front, ask you to preach. John, there might be someone in that congregation waiting to hear about Jesus through you."

Well, John couldn't say no to that, and the following Wednesday night, he and Ruth drove over to Centerville Road to meet Sister Casey.

John bought a new suit for that visit, though he wasn't sure why. Perhaps he just wanted to put his best foot forward. Sister Casey's larger church had a more affluent membership and enjoyed well-known visiting preachers. With his Bible under his arm and holding Ruth's hand, he walked into the sanctuary and had barely passed the vestibule when Sister Casey spotted them.

"Are you Brother John? Don't tell me. I know. God's telling me you're a preacher."

"Well, He told you right. I'm John Yeager, and I do a little sharing of the Word."

"John, my throat's a little scratchy tonight. Would you take the service?"

"Yes, ma'am. I'd be mighty glad to do that."

He and Ruth headed over to sit on a front pew, but Sister Casey intervened.

"John. Come on up on the stage. If you're up here during the song service, it'll be easier to give the crowd to you when I finish the introduction."

He sat up there beaming, as proud as he could be. Ruth beamed as people were whispering about who he might be. John experienced a grand moment, and Paul's words echoed in his mind, *Study to show thyself worthy*.

He studied the people, their dress, their demeanor, their actions. He scrutinized everything going on in that room, and in minutes, he noticed a young guy—about John's age or maybe a year or two older—come in.

Blond hair, blue eyes, and a dark tan that only comes from time enjoying the sun. When he moved his arms, his muscles reminded John of tiny mice running up and down under a sheet. He had a square jaw and long hair oiled straight back. He probably used Brylcreme, A little dab'll do ya! It was popular at the time; John had a dab or two on his hair as well.

A Fender guitar dangled from the guy's shoulder, and back in his sinning days, John would have called him a surfer boy—a big put-down if you come from Louisiana.

He walked directly to Sister Casey, and John overheard him say he would take care of the song service. He was impressive to look at, and John knew he would be equally impressive to hear. Without any introduction or preparation at all, he stepped on the stage, already singing.

A hush fell over the crowd. He exhibited total ease and, in less than five minutes, had everyone eating out of his hand, especially the ladies. He would flex his muscles and smile one of those Elvis smiles, and people almost swooned. As John watched him, he realized the fellow was an act—a really good one, but still an act. John felt uncomfortable but reminded himself, in these meetings, the preacher was the real deal, so no need to worry. *He was the preacher, the real deal.*

About half an hour into his show, the guy sang a song called *God's Big Tears*, which he announced as "*You can call it rain if you want to, but I call it God's Big Tears.*"

The crowd melted. People were crying. Men, women, and children sang along, shouted amen and prayed aloud. As smooth as silk, he went into a tale about Samson and Delilah. "A young man, Samson. Good looking. Every parent's dream. Every woman's dream. But more than that, he was God's dream."

"Amen." The crowd cheered. The young man continued, "He was radiant. He was mighty. God bestowed special favor on Samson, herculean strength. He wrestled a lion, slew a thousand Philistines with the jawbone of an ass, and destroyed God's enemies with a wave of his hand."

"Hallelujah. Praise the Lord."

This young man mesmerized the crowd as he talked about Samson with fervor, faith, and dramatic gestures.

"And what did God ask from him? Just following the rules: letting his hair grow, drinking no alcohol and avoiding the devil's women. But he let God down. Have you let God down?"

By this time, the audience looked at this young man as Samson incarnate. He broke into another song, and everyone joined in. John wondered *if Jesus had gotten to church yet.* The building rocked with a human-inspired commotion, and the temperature had reached a hundred degrees or better. This was the act he had to follow. This was "*the act*" he was to follow.

He planned to talk about the Day of Pentecost, Acts 2:4: "All of them were filled with the Holy Spirit and began to speak in other tongues, as the Spirit enabled them." An "action sermon" that typically produced a good crowd reaction. Souls could be saved in that atmosphere. But John felt something else in the air and heard a different voice in his heart.

As if a curtain had been raised, John suddenly saw the situation with new eyes. Sister Casey had scheduled him as Act Two of a scripted show, like a Hollywood film. Samson's goal did not include feeding his soul or anyone else's. Samson prepared the crowd for a show that ended with most people feeling good and opening their wallets. John thought about Paul.

Paul, in his visit to Athens, wanted to talk about his God, but the law forbade speaking of new gods. John wanted to save souls, not perform to fill someone else's pockets. Paul wandered through the city, looking at the statues of all the idols the people worshipped. He found a temple dedicated to "The Unknown God," and he revealed The Unknown God to be his. John found his answer in those scriptures.

When the singing and shouting and the first passing of baskets ended Act One, John stepped up to the pulpit. He spoke of the real God, the One who meets you where you are. He doesn't judge you by how high you jump or whether you speak in tongues. His love is not deterred by nicotine or alcohol. He's not preparing a lake of fire for those who make mistakes or wander into unhappy lives. The devils in this world are man-made, and it's up to man to eradicate them.

He told the crowd that God was there for them, but He's not a whipping boy to take the blame for the ills in the world. He's not there to be used as a miracle cure, to smite our enemies nor promote our friends. He is not our enemies' enemy; nor is He our friends' friend. He is God.

The crowd had quieted considerably as he went on to say, "There is a peace that passes all understanding, and that peace comes with knowing yourself and being true to your best self. It comes from accepting responsibility for who you are and where you are. It comes from accepting, forgiving, and loving yourself." That's what John told those people that night on Centerville Road.

Although the crowd was nice to him and thanked him repeatedly for his message, he was never invited back to speak at Sister Casey's church. Any curiosity as to whether his message touched any hearts was drowned out by how good he felt while trying. That night, he made a promise to himself and to God to truly get to know who he was and to find out if he liked what he found.

At long last, he understood what Paul meant when he said, "Study to show thyself worthy."

* * *

It didn't take a rocket scientist to know John was physically fit (he used no alcohol, and preaching involved quite a workout), but he was emotionally sick in that religion had taken over his life. He needed to get a grip on things, to realize that there is a balance in life. Nature has a balance. All life has balance.

Religion must have a balance.

He added studying life all around him to studying his Bible. He discovered that all people are teachers, all are students, all are preachers, and all are worshippers. It doesn't matter how high any person goes or what their position is in life; how they live their life is a sermon to those around them and to the rest of the world. Religion is a great and wonderful thing, but it is better and more wonderful when combined with knowing who you are, what you are and where you are going.

The more John learned about the answers to those questions, the more he realized you can become intertwined with God and nature and this world to form a perfect balance, or at the very least, a balance to strive for.

Picking up a hurt puppy or putting an arm around a lonely kid may be your most important job today. Taking advantage of opportunities to live your faith takes precedence over preaching your faith because it is the real message you have to offer to the world. The only authentic measure of a man's worth is not his religion but how he lives his life.

Love trumps guilt as motivation, and peace descends when we realize we are worthy.

John went to church and continued to preach, off and on, for a couple of years, and during those years he continued to study himself, his Bible, and the world around him. More importantly, he climbed one step closer to listening for that small, still voice that defines every one of us—that voice his mom had explained to him so many years ago. A church in Garland invited him to preach, and he did; another in Rowlett invited him, and he agreed. But his sermons didn't fit the program as well as they had in the past when the congregations 'amens' shook the walls. Now he talked more about living a balanced life, allowing room for so much more than just 'religion'. Eventually, he stopped delivering them.

The peace that passes all understanding is ready and waiting for anyone willing to make the effort to study and to listen to that small still voice of conscience, of God, of love and saving Grace.

CHAPTER
THREE

Sucked into a Job!

To evaluate a man's worth is not to know his religion but to watch how he lives his life.

While spreading the Word allowed him to find some peace and determine his character, his quest was not over. He, just like every person, faced precarious situations that ultimately allowed him to dig a little deeper into his psyche in search of himself.

On a warm Saturday morning in 1966, John sat in a lawn chair perusing a newspaper while he drank coffee. Married and working for minimum wage, he felt older than his twenty-one years. Things were tough, and the want ads were of particular interest. As he flipped through the newspaper something appeared, and it felt like manna from heaven.

> HELP WANTED. Must be able to get along on $99.50 a week for the first three weeks!

His entire being lit up! His current take-home pay, after taxes and whatever else they deducted, amounted to $30 or $32 a week. Minimum wage totaled $1.35 per hour in those days. But $99.50 a week! Good times were at his fingertips, and he said a quiet prayer as he entered his house at a fast trot to grab the phone.

"Hello. I'm John Yeager, and I'm calling about that help-wanted ad in the *Times Herald*. That job still open?"

"Yessir. Still is. Why don't you come on down, and let's talk."

"Today? It's Saturday."

"That's right, sir. If you want a chance at this job, you need to show up now."

John got the address and directions. He rushed to change clothes. In less than an hour, he jumped into his car and headed across town. It didn't take long to find the main address, but looking for the office required more time than expected.

A single door beckoned him with a sign: Stratton Vacuum Cleaners—Sales. He walked in to find a short man dressed in a suit with his hair slicked back, looking prosperous, seated in a large plush office chair.

John stood still. He felt nervous, but before he could overcome his hesitancy, the man stood up as if he were excited to see John.

"Come on in."

The man extended his *soft-as-a-feather-pillow* hand, and John reciprocated. The hand he shook did not have a blemish anywhere, and John felt embarrassed by his own rough calluses. Still, he vigorously shook the man's hand. After all, his dad's voice echoed in his head with a saying he had told him a million times: *You can tell a lot about a man by how he shakes your hand.*

"I'm John Yeager. I talked to one of your fellows on the phone." He paused and took a deep breath. "I'm here about that $99.50 a week job. Your man on the phone said you will train a fellow."

"Training is free." He turned and looked toward an open office door. "Hey, Frank, come out here. I think we have us a natural." He turned back to John. "Shake this man's hand."

John then shook hands with the other fellow and got a big reaction from him as well.

"This boy's a natural, Ed."

The men were on either side of him, arms around his shoulders, as they led him into the office.

John's thoughts were all over the place, but without a doubt, he knew: *This is my lucky day!*

Getting a job on a handshake might sound like a fairy tale, but these guys seemed so genuine and impressed, John didn't question his luck for even a minute. They talked a little, laughed a little and finally, one of them mentioned getting a bite to eat.

"Hey, John, do you have time to have some lunch, and then we can talk some more?"

"Well, I do. But I'm running a little short on cash today."

"Oh, no! We'll buy lunch. It's not every day a *natural* walks through those doors." Ed gestured at the same time Frank was walking out.

Once in the parking lot, they guided him to a Cadillac. John's feet barely touched the ground as he realized the importance of being a *natural.* Ed's and Frank's questions peppered him all during Luby's Cafeteria lunch.

"What are you doing for a living, now, John?"

"I work for the City of Garland. I'm a trainee in the water department."

"Experience dealing with the public?"

"No, sir. My job is mainly manual labor, digging out leaks, that sort of thing. I don't deal directly with the public."

"Well, that's a shame, you being a *natural* and everything."

Ed and Frank took a minute to look at John and then at each other. A Christmas morning surprise could not have matched the pleasure John observed in their eyes. He beamed back at them.

"You know, fellows, I never knew I was a *natural*."

Both guys chuckled as they simultaneously stood up. Frank said, "John, it's rare. Just glad you came in. Let's get on back to the office so we can talk business."

Back at the office, John learned they needed a man to sell vacuum cleaners. The first three weeks would consist of a training period to determine if John could pass the test.

Ed explained, "John, as a natural, you won't have any trouble learning the skills that will make you rich. You'll be given all the sales techniques, from openings to closings. By the end of the three weeks, I expect you to be top of the class. With your natural ability, selling is secondary. You just share what you know, and the cleaners will sell themselves."

"I don't know about that. It all sounds a bit over my head." John continued to radiate the surprise and disbelief one might have if he had been told he had won the million-dollar lottery.

"Well, you ought to give it a try. At $99.50 a week, what do you have to lose, other than your minimum wage job?"

Then Frank spoke up with a reassuring smile. "Let me give you your first lesson right now."

"Awright."

"Forget the word vacuum. You make Stratton Cleaners available to the people who need them. Nobody at Stratton ever wants to hear any salesperson call those cleaners vacuums. Think you can remember that?"

"Well, yessir, but is that a lesson?"

"Your first one! Your next one will be Monday morning at eight o'clock . . . if we get this paperwork completed now."

"Hold on. I can't just not show up at my job on Monday." John liked the people he worked with, and walking out without notice seemed a bit underhanded.

With a look of shock, both men spoke at once. "For $99.50?"

John signed on.

Monday morning, he got up earlier than usual. Getting dressed felt like an event, a new beginning in a world of success and one he had to get precisely right. He found his best pair of blue jeans, cleaned his work boots, and practiced getting his hair combed back as near as possible to the style sported by both Frank and Ed. He left the house looking as sharp as he could. Convinced in his heart that he had hit the big time, he was eager to open the door to opportunity.

He arrived early, at about 7:30 a.m. Again, his dad's voice whispered in his mind, *Get there early, son. Show initiative."*

He entered and scanned the large room. About fifteen men stood around, drinking coffee and talking. Seeing so many boosted his confidence. Excitement filled the air, like the electrical charge in a stormy sky. The primary topic among the men appeared to be the $99.50 Frank and Ed were willing to pay each one of them, practical strangers, just for showing up for three weeks.

The atmosphere alone made John's skin tingle. That tingle swung from euphoria to a *hair-on-the back-of-your-neck-feeling*. He stood to the side and quietly thought about the conversations he had with Frank and Ed: "*You are a natural.*" He had gotten the job based solely on a handshake. I bet the others had to do more to prove themselves.

He wandered over to a short, stocky guy dressed like himself. He looked friendly, and a chat broke out over coffee. They exchanged names and where they were from. Then John asked, "Elton, will you share your hiring experience with me?"

"I've never had a day like that in my life! This big guy, I think his name is Frank—I know it's Frank and Ed, but I'm not sure I remember who's who. Anyway, we shook hands, and my life changed.

"Did you go to Luby's?"

"I did. You know, I have no sales experience and don't know if I will ever sell a vacuum cleaner. Frankly, I don't care if I even get trained. $99.50 a week to come down here and listen to these guys. Well, I wasn't doing anything else anyway. In three weeks, I'll make more than I was making in three months!"

John opened his mouth to reply just as the instructor sort of leaped into the room, immediately drawing all eyes to him. He looked sharp, wearing a suit that shouted expensive. His shoes shone so that every student who looked down saw their reflection looking back. He carried a large box with him. He placed it at the side of the stage, carefully covered it with a sheet, and then bounced to the front of the room. John thought the instructor must have trained in a *bouncy house* and smiled. The students stood, stared, and waited for their turn to join the fun.

After a rather extended period, their leader occupied center stage and grabbed the microphone.

"Sit down, gentlemen, and prepare to get rich." He flipped on a film and walked out.

Still appearing to be in a bit of a trance, the students now sat and watched the Don Ameche film. It was so quiet, a pin dropping would be heard. Hypnotism came to John's mind as he continued to listen to every word Don Ameche spoke.

He defined cold canvassing. John, not sure he had ever heard the term, listened carefully. The gist of the explanation was that they would be going into neighborhoods and knocking on doors. The homeowner would answer, and they would tell them about the product.

One Don Ameche sentence stuck in John's mind:

"There has never been a sale made until you have knocked on one million doors."

Dadgum, how can these guys pay each of us $99.50 every week to go into unknown neighborhoods and knock on doors, knowing all the while it could take a million to make a sale? While it seemed strange to John, and he felt a few hairs' warning, he continued to listen eagerly to every one of Don Ameche's words.

Don talked about how to look at people, how to move and what props are most helpful. "Every salesman needs to carry a pair of glasses with him. Put those glasses on when you talk about the cleaner. When you make a point, take the glasses off and lay them down—on a table, on a mantle—just so they are nearby."

Don showed them how to do that, several times, using suggested gestures, turning a certain way, smiling, not smiling, glasses on, glasses off, etc. This went on for fifteen or twenty minutes. It seemed silly to John, *but if that's what they want, I'll buy a pair of glasses, first thing.*

At the end of the first film, Frank entered and walked directly to the podium, scanned all the faces in the room, and began talking.

"First of all, I want to thank each of you for showing up this morning and for being on time. Being on time is important. If you have an appointment, you should plan on being fifteen minutes early every time.

His eyes met those of each individual candidate. "Men, you are the best group of candidates I've had the pleasure of meeting. We will be the most successful team ever."

He nodded in the direction of his audience as if making a covenant with each man. No one could doubt his eagerness or his passion. Electricity was in the air, and John, along with the rest of the class, began to feel special. Suddenly, Frank went completely silent. As if a radio turned off, everyone followed suit. The air seemed to be sucked out of the room and replaced with an otherworldly and spellbinding commodity.

John thought, *This is more than a job. This is a calling.* For a moment he even considered he was being hypnotized. Whatever it was, $99.50 a week held his attention.

While every man there immersed himself in the mysterious new surroundings, thirty seconds—maybe a full minute—of complete and palpable silence permeated the room.

Without warning, Frank spoke again. "I've got someone here who is eager to meet each of you. He's your field counselor, and his responsibility is to share with you the finer points of Stratton Cleaners. He's the first step to financial freedom. Let's give him a big hand."

Frank started to clap, quickly joined by the entire class.

The field counselor, Al, danced in with an ear-to-ear smile. He was a short, lightweight fellow, pushing five feet, six inches tall, and conceivably weighing 135 pounds soaking wet. He wore dress pants, a sports coat, and an open-collared shirt. He looked a little nerdy with his horn-rimmed glasses and slightly protruding front teeth.

The energy of his entrance contradicted the nerd vibe his appearance portrayed. He came out dancing, looking like an off-brand rock 'n' roll act about to begin. He made a couple of turns, slid across the stage, looking *I-got-the-last-cookie-happy*, then he grabbed the podium like a painter with a fresh canvas ready to create a masterpiece.

In a *pin-drop-quiet* room, John and his classmates waited for the next step in today's training.

"My name is Al, and I'm your field counselor."

His smile disappeared, replaced with his dead-serious face as he glanced from person to person. No one said a word, and those few seconds of silence were hypnotic. Not a man moved or spoke.

Then he shouted, "NOT BUY!"

With the shout, every man moved; indeed, most nearly jumped out of their seats. Still, as a group, they remained quiet and focused on Al. His stare and the strange look on his face held his class's complete focus. Could he be waiting for response or inspiration? To a man, the class sat like a blank canvas waiting for the artist to add his magic.

"SELL!"

Al yelled as loudly as possible. The class continued to stare, as if frozen in time. Al repeated this performance four or five times before all the guys stood up and began to respond to his "not buy" with their "sell."

This went on until they reached a fever pitch and Al stopped yelling.

Again, the silence set in, and Al indicated they were to take a seat and look at the pamphlets on their seat. *On their seat?* No one believed there was anything on their seats. They had stood directly in front of their chairs. But there it was: every seat had a three- or four-page leaflet and every face looked as if they had seen a ghost—or rather had not seen the ghost! By this time, the impossible had entered the realm of possible. John joined his classmates in picking up the brochure to discover a songbook with songs written to the tunes of various old-time gospel songs.

Al announced, "Everyone look at page one—'That Good Ol' Stratton Feeling' sung to the tune of 'That Old Time Religion.'"

The class sang that song multiple times, as well as a half-dozen other tunes that created something of a religious cult atmosphere. John was in familiar territory now. He knew the value of songs and the ambiance they could add to any meeting.

As they sang, Al moved among them, shook every hand, and welcomed each of them personally to the new group of Stratton Cleaner salespeople. The clock struck twelve noon. With the same enthusiasm he brought to the room hours earlier, Al bounced onto the stage with more words of wisdom.

"It's been quite a morning. I want each of you to shake the hand of every other man in this room. I want you to share your feelings. You are now members of the Stratton team, but it's going to take some effort to remain members. The Stratton team is exclusive, and only the best qualify as lifetime members. I believe in each of you." He slowly surveyed the room, connecting with every student's eye, like a lighthouse guiding the lost ship to a safe port.

"Take a lunch break." He smiled. "Be back here in one hour, and I will introduce you to the product that will make you rich."

John had brought his lunch, as had about two-thirds of the class. Settling into small groups at various tables, the men automatically formed teams of like thinkers as they ate and waited for session two.

Al walked out of the room.

To the best of his memory, this was the first time at any job, John felt eager to get back to work. An expectant feeling permeated the entire room. Like runners poised in the starting blocks, all the class members settled in their seats ten minutes before one o'clock, ready for the race to begin.

Al walked in looking as fresh and as exuberant as he had when he left. A quiet fell over the room as he took the stage. He floated over to the sheet-covered box and removed that sheet with the care of an artist unveiling a priceless painting for the first time.

He opened the top and meticulously lifted out five unassembled vacuum pieces, placing each one on the floor in front of him. He then took out the cord and swung it as a cowboy would swing a lariat over his head, roping one unassembled piece and dancing the entire time. He stopped suddenly and turned to face his students.

"The Stratton Cleaner has a thirty-two-foot cord. Did you know that? A thirty-two-foot cord. Remember that. It's important. A thirty-two-foot cord."

Then, Al set about putting the cleaner together, talking nonstop as if he were selling it to the class. When he finished, John, with no money in his pocket, wanted to buy that Stratton Cleaner—on the spot. Every member of the class shared his fascination with the machine. John had never seen anything like it. The Stratton Cleaner looked like an ordinary vacuum cleaner, perhaps a little sturdier, but this machine was far from ordinary. The more Al told them that, the more they believed it.

The class watched Al assemble and disassemble the Stratton Cleaner for the rest of the day (with a couple of fifteen- or twenty-minute breaks). Every performance included a sales spiel, basically the same words and the same demonstration, with just enough nuance of change to keep the students' interest.

At about four thirty Al stopped, turned to the class, and said, "I'll see you at eight a.m. tomorrow." With that, he left the room.

John sat there still mesmerized for a couple of minutes. All the way home, he wondered what he had gotten into and if there really would be a $99.50 check on Friday. He considered the pros and cons of that first payday. By the time he got home, he had mentally paid all his bills.

For the next three days, John showed up at 7:50 a.m., along with fifteen of the original sixteen other recruited Stratton team members. Tuesday and Wednesday were repeats of Monday, from the sales pitch through singing to vacuum assemblies. The class was now fully engaged in the routine; some would suggest a particular song; the braver ones would step up to assemble a cleaner; others might shout out "NOT BUY!" to which the rest of the class would respond "SELL!"

A couple of students even stepped up to imitate Don Ameche's performance. The three days went by quickly, and the classroom held a closer-knit group than the men who walked in the door on day one. All were excited and spent their lunch hours mentally spending that first $99.50.

On Thursday morning, they arrived expecting more of the same and looking forward to that $99.50 Friday paycheck. Thursday began much like Tuesday and Wednesday until Al said they would be working in teams. He brought in his own partner, Bob, and the two of them worked together on the sales routine. Then the class members paired up, and Al explained the team approach to a sale. He referred to the homeowners who would open the doors as Chester and Agnes and, of course, the team member who portrayed the salesman was one of the students who used their own names.

Interestingly enough, a second member had dropped out, so now they had exactly fourteen, creating seven teams. By the end of that day, John loved the Stratton Cleaner; he could put it together as easily as Al did, and his sales pitch was just as fluid. That night he barely slept, eager to get that $99.50 on Friday.

At 7:50 a.m. the students, filled with a bit of anxiety, sat in the classroom, and waited for Al to show up. The atmosphere resembled Christmas Eve with five-year-old kids waiting for Santa. The feeling of expectation and optimism bounced from student to student along with the nagging doubt about receiving that prized gift of $99.50 and the possibility that Al might not show up.

Al eventually showed up, and the day was a carbon copy of the last four days. The excitement created a competitive feel, and the skill with which they did their jobs grew as the day wore on. By the time they hit the second break after lunch, every man in that room allowed his imagination to take over and had spent his $99.50.

At 4 p.m., Al made an announcement. "Okay, guys. We're done for the week." His Cheshire Cat smile quieted the room. "Go home, get plenty of rest, and we'll see you at 8 a.m. on Monday."

John was depending on that check, but he didn't want to look needy or dumb. He thought, *Maybe on these kinds of jobs, the paycheck comes differently*. He glanced around the room to see everyone else looking disgruntled. No one looked angry, but more as if they had been hit in the stomach and were trying to catch their breath.

Al bounced around from person to person, telling them how well they had done that week. He stuck his hand out, and every one of those students put their hand on top of his. He yelled, "NOT BUY!" The students yelled back, "SELL!" Still, John noticed a bit less enthusiasm than usual in the "sell."

By 4:15 p.m. on that first Friday afternoon, all the team members had left the building except for John and his new buddy, Elton.

"Elton, I really need a paycheck today."

"So do I, John. I'm in a tight spot. I saw those two guys who hired us go into that room up the hall."

"Let's go talk to them. At least we can ask them how paychecks work with this job. They might mail it to us or something. I'm trying to remember that ad we answered. Do you remember exactly what it said?"

"I don't either. I don't remember it saying we would be paid on Friday, just that weekly pay during training was $99.50."

At about that time, Al, and Bob walked by and into the room up the hall. John and Elton agreed their best bet was to go into that same room. As they approached the doorway, they heard laughing and talking. Although they could not hear exactly what the men were saying, it increased their resolve. As they reached the doorway, they paused as all four guys were having beers. With their backs turned toward the door, they faced a city map hung on the wall, pointing and talking while checking papers.

Al was the first to notice John and Elton. The look on his face didn't resemble any they had observed while in class. The other three turned and shared equally obvious looks of annoyance but said nothing.

John spoke first. "Al, I need my paycheck. I thought I would be paid today, and I have a family to feed. How does this all work?"

Elton added his appeal. "You know, guys, when I showed up for this job, you knew I was broke. I've borrowed money to get to payday. What do I do now?"

Al's countenance changed into one of concern. He threw his arms around both John and Elton and led them back out into the corridor, down the hall and to the front doorway. He talked every step of the way.

"Boys, you've got two more weeks of training to go. If we paid everyone today, how many wouldn't show up on Monday? We have already lost two."

It occurred to John that this was not Al's first rodeo. "Well, I would show up."

"I know you two would. You're both naturals, and when you complete this training, you'll make more money than you have ever seen."

"But I need something now. What about this week?"

"John, don't think about this week. This week is over. Think about all the money you will make when you start selling Stratton Cleaners! You know, it is not us who are holding your money. It's Chester and Agnes. Give it two more weeks, and you'll start collecting from them."

With that, they were at the front door. Elton and John looked at each other. They stood silently for about thirty seconds or so and then said in unison: "See ya, Monday."

For two more weeks, John showed up every day at 7:50 a.m.

The class put those cleaners together, took them apart. They worked with their partners; they changed partners; they worked with Al; they worked with Bob. They watched Don Ameche films. John learned all the right comebacks to whatever Chester and Agnes might say. John could counter any objection with a scripted answer, feeling prepared and eager to hit the streets.

On the last Friday of training, the whole class, which was now down to just twelve students, spent the entire day singing, clapping their hands, and having a good time. Every so often, someone would shout, "NOT BUY!" and the rest of the group would answer, "SELL!"

Around three that afternoon, Al told them that, come Monday morning, they would begin collecting what Chester and Agnes owed them. Two evenly divided groups, one under Al's leadership and the other directed by Bob, were sorted as Al shared his last wisdom of the week with them.

"I want each one of you to spend the weekend thinking about what you have learned over the past three weeks. Replay in your mind the openings, the objections, and the closings you have learned. Remember, Chester and Agnes have your money, and your job is to help them understand that."

Someone laughed, and Al turned to stare at him with a stony lack of any humor. John glanced to see who could be so disrespectful, and he nodded when Al replied to the outburst.

"It is our job as Stratton Cleaner salespeople to educate Chester and Agnes. They must learn that the only way to be good, respectable citizens is to sign that contract. Stratton Cleaners are the only way to have clean homes—as God intended them to be—for clean people. We are missionaries of cleanliness, and we know that is God's teaching."

An evangelistic air engulfed the scene. John felt a wave of confidence. He had found the path to financial freedom doing a job he believed in. So, why was that confidence shaken by a slight shiver that ran up his back?

John spent the weekend practicing what he had learned. He role-played with his wife, even to the point of knocking on the door.

"Hello, ma'am. I would like to show you a Stratton Cleaner."

"Not interested," Ruth, as Agnes, said as she closed the door.

"Ma'am, give me just one minute. I'm not here to sell you a cleaner. I just want to show it to you."

"What do you mean? I don't need a vacuum." She lightened up, and a smile crossed her face.

"Of course, you don't, and I'm not here to sell you one." He put on his most concerned expression. "To tell you the truth, ma'am, I am looking for somebody who will help me, help a buddy of mine."

Agnes, in the form of Ruth, behaved exactly as Al said she would. She relaxed, repeating the script statement, and the atmosphere immediately changed in John's favor.

"What do you mean: *help a buddy?*"

"I overheard my big boss, Mr. McCandless, tell my field supervisor that a buddy of mine will be fired today unless he shows at least one Stratton Cleaner. He really needs this job, and I want to help him. He's got kids. Let me show you this cleaner, and I'll put his name on the slip. Takes about twenty minutes. Then I'm outta here."

John stood while Agnes considered the request. His final word was, "Please."

That scenario was a last resort spiel, and it would work if properly performed; it was also the presentation with which John was the least comfortable. The plan required John to put the Stratton box on the porch as part of the ruse to help a buddy. Al, cruising the neighborhood, would see the box, knock on the door, and show the salesperson how to close the sale.

But somewhere in his mind, it didn't feel right, and he never expected to use it. Of course, it was always better to have an ace in the hole than to be totally alone.

* * *

John was treading water in dire financial straits by now. The City of Garland had held back one check, and that helped, but for the last two weeks he had lived on credit—credit from the landlord, credit from the gas station, credit from the neighborhood store, credit from everybody.

He thought sleep would never come on that last Sunday night before the curtain went up on his new life on Monday morning. He worried about his inability to smooth-talk strangers, but Al and Bob reminded him he was natural. They explained many times, his way of talking made a sale when the best smooth talker around could not.

He remembered Al's final words:

"John, you were not hired to sell the Stratton Cleaners. You were hired to show the cleaners. The Stratton Cleaners sell themselves."

With that thought in mind, John fell asleep to dream of his new life.

He got to the office early Monday morning, but he did not claim the first spot in line. Instead, he stood behind several fellow graduates already waiting. Everyone was eager to get started, and the mood remained light as they loaded into two old black Chevy vans outfitted with school bus seats. John occupied the van Al drove. As he climbed in, the thought of the Cadillac used for lunch three weeks ago crossed his mind, but only briefly.

Soon, singing and clapping filled the van and continued all the way to the neighborhood chosen for that day's event. The plan seemed almost too simple: Al picked various street corners to drop off one guy and a cleaner. That guy would walk up one side of the street and down the other, knocking on every door. If he didn't get in, he would be standing on the corner, with the cleaner, waiting for the van when Al cruised by.

One of the more astute guys spoke up before he got out of the van.

"Hey, Al. Don't I need a solicitor's permit to knock on doors in this neighborhood?"

"No, sir. We're in Dallas, and Dallas doesn't require a solicitor's permit. Sometimes the cops do get a little fussy. If that happens, just call the number on this paper."

He handed each of them a business-card-sized note with a phone number written on it.

"Where will we call you from?"

Al smiled slightly. "If the police get pushy, it'll be from the police station. It won't cost you anything, and someone will be there in a jiffy. They'll straighten out the whole matter."

Then Al moved swiftly into the business of the day.

"Remember, you will make sixty dollars on each of the first seven Stratton Cleaners you sell today and one hundred twenty dollars on number eight. Are you ready?"

He yelled, "NOT BUY!"

Every man in the van yelled back, "SELL!"

Shaking like a leaf, John stepped from the van at the next corner. He had his Stratton Cleaner and a silverware set in his hand. The silverware was the gift he would give Chester and Agnes for the privilege of letting him show his Stratton Cleaner; the $5.95 tag was still on the box, and he made certain it was visible.

Like a broken record, his planned opening played and replayed in his mind: *I'm only asking for twenty minutes, and I'm willing to pay $5.95 for it.*

The first door he knocked on opened, and he walked in like an innocent lamb to slaughter. Still, in the back of his mind, he felt as safe as a turtle inside its shell. He knew what to do, what to say and when to do it.

"Good morning. I know you think I am a salesperson—but you'll be surprised to discover I am only here to show this vacuum. Have you got twenty minutes I can buy for $5.95?" He barely took a breath.

"Chester" and "Agnes" stared blankly as they stepped aside and John entered.

Wearing his extra-confident look and the glasses he had managed to borrow, he attached the dirt meter to the Stratton Cleaner. He smiled, removed the glasses, and pointed at the electric broom.

"This is going to blow you away," he said with another smile as he began his demonstration in the kitchen.

Agnes watched every move as he went through the complete kitchen demonstration. She even asked a question or two and offered a few compliments. Chester sat quietly; his only reaction occurred when John turned off his TV set.

"Chester, you don't mind if we turn off the TV, do you? The $5.95 silverware set buys you and your wife's time for twenty minutes. I would be in trouble if my supervisor found out I was just giving it away." Again, he used his *I-need-you* look.

Agnes chimed in to help seal the deal. "Come on, honey. I want that silverware set, and we're only talking about twenty minutes."

Chester joined them, though not so enthusiastically.

At the end of the presentation, Agnes put her hand on his arm in an almost motherly way.

"John, I'm impressed with you and with your machine, but we're not in a position to purchase a vacuum cleaner today."

"Ma'am, I'm not in a position to *sell* you a vacuum cleaner today. This, ma'am, is not a vacuum cleaner. It's a Stratton Cleaner. There's a big difference—"

Before he could finish his sentence, Agnes interrupted him with a rather firm, but kind look in her eye. "I'm sorry, son, but we can't do it."

Chester made his way back toward his recliner in front of the TV while John silently ran through the various spiels he had learned over the last three weeks. He decided to use his Stratton National Bank close.

As Agnes stood her ground, slightly smiling but still firm, John removed three dimes from his pocket and dropped them one at a time into the handle of the Stratton Cleaner. Then he looked at Agnes as if he had just sunk the three-pointer to win the NBA championship.

"Do that every day, Agnes, and there's your payment at the end of the month."

"It's not just the money, John. We don't need a vacuum cleaner."

Not to be deterred, John walked toward the husband. He pulled out his front money, the twenty dollars given to each team member that morning to be returned at the end of the day, meant to be used in a closing if necessary.

He laid the twenty-dollar bill on the coffee table and stood by like a fisherman waiting for the big one to take the bait. After about fifteen seconds of silence and no reaction from Chester, he spoke again.

"Chester, if I buy your wife a new dress, will you talk to me about this cleaner?"

Chester did not hesitate. "Nope. Put your twenty back in your pocket. We don't want a vacuum cleaner today. You need to move on, son."

"Okay. No pressure from me. I've done my job by showing the cleaner to you."

John looked as pleasant as possible, shook hands with Chester, and thanked them for their time. He began packing up his stuff, then stopped for just a moment and looked up at Agnes, cocking his head to one side. As if it were an afterthought, he said, "Agnes, I do have a buddy who needs some help."

"I've met a lot of people in my time, and I know you're a caring, Christian woman. I just *know* it; I *feel it*, and I would be remiss if I didn't tell you about my friend."

As he continued to pack up his stuff, he launched into his *buddy-about-to-be-fired* story. Chester and Agnes talked quietly to each other. Agnes really wanted to help John's buddy, and she finally got Chester on board.

"We'll listen to you, son, but we need to see this buddy of yours." Chester laughed a bit as he added, with some sarcasm, "I might not be as *Christian* and *caring* as my wife. I need to see your buddy. Can you get in touch with him?"

John joined Chester in the laugh. "Yes, sir, I think I can. We are both in your neighborhood. I think he saw me come up onto your porch." John walked over to the door and stepped outside briefly. He looked both ways, as if hoping to see his buddy.

"Well, maybe he's inside, and everything's okay. I'm going to set this box out here while I finish packing up. If he sees it, he might come over. We've used it as a signal before."

John set the box on the porch, went back inside and began to sweat a bit. He felt about as popular as a fly at a picnic. He stood near the door, ready to walk out when the knock sounded.

Chester let Al in. John felt like the cavalry had arrived. Al smiled, shook everyone's hands, and, without another word, hooked up his dirt meter and began his presentation.

He showed them how much dirt there was right in front of their couch. He asked them what kind of cleaner had failed to clean this spot.

Agnes answered, "It's a Hoover. A very nice one."

"Where do you keep it?"

"In the hall closet. Why?"

Al walked over to the closet, took out the Hoover, and made about twenty swipes in one spot. Chester and Agnes stood there, staring. Then Al got his Stratton Cleaner and vacuumed that same spot. He held the dirt meter in front of Agnes.

"Agnes, look at this dirt meter. Do you let your children play on this carpet at night?"

"Well, yes. They watch TV sitting there sometimes."

"After they have bathed?"

"Yes."

Al appeared to be horrified. John watched in fascination as the scene played out.

"You may as well allow them to play in the dirt outside. Outside dirt is cleaner than the filth in this carpet. There's no sunshine, no air to prevent all kinds of germs from growing in this carpet." His brows knit into a deep frown. "Agnes, you're taking a chance with your children's health every day."

Agnes stood there, not saying a word or making a move, but her face revealed her embarrassment and a touch of shame.

From there, Al moved on to the kitchen demonstration, using the electric broom. Standing in front of the stove, he put a white cloth napkin on the floor. He stepped on the napkin, twisted, went down on one knee as he pretended to fall. He put on quite a show as his audience stood spellbound.

Finally, he picked up the napkin full of greasy dirt.

"Look at this, Agnes. I know any food that hits this floor is immediately thrown out."

As he laid the napkin on the counter, he threw them a disgusted grimace. He turned on the Stratton Cleaner with the electric broom and ran it over that same spot, smiling all the while. Then he took out another white cloth napkin.

"I'm going to do the twist one more time," he said, laughing. No one else made a sound.

He stood on the napkin and provided a less vigorous performance, only about fifteen or twenty seconds long, this time. Both Chester and Agnes stared at the napkin. Then he picked it up and held it in front of Agnes for her to see how little, if any, grease, or dirt was on it. John was impressed as he realized it was Agnes' turn to sweat a little. She radiated the attitude of a chicken seeing a fox in the henhouse and trying to determine the best exit.

She had a different attitude toward Al than she had toward John. Chester returned to the recliner following the kitchen demonstration. As Al, Agnes and John joined Chester in the living room, Al took a piece of rubber out of his pocket. *A new prop.* One John had not seen before. He watched carefully, and even Chester seemed fascinated.

Al turned the rubber thing inside out. "Mr. Stratton did not know what to name this thing, so we just call it a gizmo. It's used for a lot of things. You can de-flea a dog with it or unstop your sink."

He paused, giving Chester a sharp look. "When was the last time you shampooed your hair, Chester?"

"Last night."

John soon learned that everyone's answer was always, "Last night."

"Mind if I try something?" Al stared at Chester's hair.

"Well, I guess. If it doesn't hurt." Chester laughed a little. "Go ahead."

That living room had been transformed into a stage for a play, or an alternate reality where everyone had a part to play. Nothing came off as too ridiculous or too foolish to be accepted as normal. Al assumed the starring role as the master, and his fellow performers also served as his audience.

Al put a black cloth into the dirt meter and began to run the gizmo over Chester's head, all the while explaining the dry shampoo used with the gizmo. He rubbed Chester's head for thirty seconds. Then he pulled off the dirt meter and laid the black cloth on the coffee table.

What a sight to see, all covered with dandruff, dirt, and loose hair.

"Are you sure, Chester, it was just *last night* that you washed your hair?" Al smiled.

"I'm sure." Chester did not smile, his brows knitted.

"I know you are, and I'm not doubting you. You just don't have a way to get your head clean or to keep it clean. I am offering you a way to get clean and to stay clean."

A small, but somewhat heated, argument began between Chester and Agnes, and while they talked, Al got out the contract. Agnes wanted that cleaner, but Chester still balked. Al turned toward both. He diverted their attention with his words.

"Agnes, you can be clean, and your house can be clean. Your children will not risk picking up germs by simply sitting on the floor in front of the TV. I know you want to be best mother, wife and house-keeper possible. How about it?"

Agnes did not say a word but quietly nodded her head. Al turned his attention to Chester.

"Chester, if I stand on my head, will you sign this contract and give me $23.95 for your first weekly payment? I'll get out of your hair. You can be clean, and your house can be clean. How about it?"

"Yeah. If you *stand on your head*, I'll do it," Chester said sarcastically, then turned to walk away.

Al shot straight up on his head, right in front of the coffee table. Coins, cigarettes, matches, car keys, everything in his pocket fell to the floor, and Al's face began to turn red. Still, he spoke from his upside-down position.

"John, hand him that contract so he can sign it."

"I ain't signing any contract," Chester snarled.

"Well, you said you would if I stood on my head."

Agnes stepped in. "Honey, you said you would, and I know how you feel about giving your word." She smiled sweetly as she put her arm around Chester's waist.

Chester signed the contract, and John's first Stratton Cleaner was sold. He made sixty dollars in less than two hours, and he learned how to sell Stratton Cleaners.

He began to experiment with his own openings to get in the door. He found it interesting to speculate as to what would work just by looking at each Chester and Agnes. He did not need to put the Stratton box outside any more doors. He knew that if he couldn't sell the cleaner, neither could Al.

He was on his way to living *the good life*. So why did that shiver run up his spine again? John shook it off as he mentally counted his future income.

He excelled at selling Stratton Cleaners. He showed up, worked hard, and made some fat checks. He paid off all his creditors, paid his landlord four months' rent in advance and bought himself a coon hound.

At twenty-one years old, he lacked self-management. Even with a wife and a baby, he often found it hard to come up with a good reason to go to work when he had extra dollars in his pocket, a place to live and food on the table. He told himself, in Al style, *I'll let Chester and Agnes hold my money until I need it.* He worked sporadically, made some sales, took a few days off to go coon hunting, play with his hound, have a beer with his buddies, or just stay home with the wife and baby, John III.

Yes, sir, he was in a good place, and by taking only what he needed, he felt somewhat entitled. He had figured out how to make a living and enjoy life at the same time. When money got low or they needed something, John grabbed his cleaner and showed up at the office at 7:50 a.m.

Sometimes, Al met him at the door. Once, he said, "John, we're going to have to cut you loose. I need to pick up your cleaner."

"Well, Al, I sell cleaners when I work."

"You're just not regular enough."

"It's too bad you showed up today, Al, because I'm ready to sell some cleaners." John shouted out, "NOT BUY!" waited a second or two and followed himself up with, "SELL!"

Al smiled and agreed to another chance. That routine happened too many times to count.

When John worked, he sold cleaners. Al even had him assist in training sessions or lend a hand to weaker students. John had been there three, maybe four, months before he had his first $540, selling eight cleaners a week. That week, combined with six- and five-cleaner weeks just before it, allowed John to enjoy life on his own terms for the next two weeks.

Then Al showed up at John's house. "John, it's over. I need your cleaner."

"Come on, Al. Let's work this out."

"You don't want to sell cleaners, or you would be at work. If you change your mind, show up, and your cleaner will be sitting right there in the office."

As he spoke, Al picked up John's cleaner, put it in the trunk of his Cadillac, slid behind the wheel, and drove away.

Beginning with the next morning, John showed up every day for a month—singing, clapping, joining in the NOT BUY . . . SELL chants as the two old Chevys set out to hit new neighborhoods. Two or three occupants, besides John, were from the original sales group, but Elton was not one of them; John missed him. The team had changed, but the routine had not.

The money was good, and John had become skilled. He had another eight-cleaner week, but something didn't fit right. He had a *rock-in-his-shoe* feeling; you know—the shoes look good, serve most of your needs, but that nagging little ache makes you uncomfortable every time you put them on.

Three of the guys, including John, were picked up by the Irving police because they did not have solicitor permits. Al came down, paid the fine and got them out. John was picked up again in Garland for the same reason, and Al came down, paid the fine and got him out.

He had seen Agnes cry and Chester get uncomfortable when he added a little religious pressure. He had a knack for turning that Stratton Cleaner into an almost-Christian symbol. He could convince Agnes and Chester of their unclean ways, showing them the filth, the dirt, and the grime in their homes. He would get on his knees in front of the TV, lay his glasses on the coffee table, and show them their dirt. Then he would look around the room. If he saw a cross, a Bible or any religious symbol, he would bring it into his spiel by saying something similar to:

"You know, Paul said cleanliness is next to holiness. Have you heard of that? Stratton Cleaners gives you an opportunity to live cleaner, better lives."

If they didn't have the money, his typical comeback created a choice between doing what was right and feeling second-class. "I don't care about the money. My goal is to save you from the filth you didn't know you were living in. But now you know. Now you are responsible for the results of that filth."

Some people got angry and told him to pack up his stuff and get out, but more than enough tried to clean up. He knew that buying it was a strain on their budgets, but his sales pitch convinced enough couples that they had a Christian duty to buy that Stratton Cleaner.

A few times he even went to jail for doing his job. Every time that happened, Al sidled into the jail, already opening his wallet while John sat on a bench watching.

"Here to pick up John Yeager."

The officer on duty smiled as if he and Al had a privately shared secret. Within minutes, they were in Al's vehicle, headed back to the neighborhood. John looked straight ahead as he spoke to Al.

"Al, do you remember that conversation we had after I made my first Straton sale?

"No, John, I don't." He sounded tired, as if that 'Not Buy, Sell' routine had drained all of his energy.

"Well, I clearly remember that wise old owl feeling I felt and enjoyed so much after that first sale. Now, that feeling is morphing into more of a cunning fox taking advantage of the henhouse chickens. He sounded as lonely and as tired as the day left Tioga years ago.

Al assumed his usual demeanor and personality, quickly erasing any tiredness. He laughed. "John, you've had a long day. Why don't you go home and relax this afternoon?"

He did go home that day and sat outside, mentally examining his life—his real feelings from deep inside: his trouble sleeping at night, the lack of joy in the mini vacations, how, in the middle of a coon hunt and having a beer with his buddies, he would suddenly imagine a Chester or an Agnes, near tears, trying to make a payment on their Stratton Cleaner.

In the end, it was his mom again who pointed the way. As he sat on the front lawn playing with his son, he could hear her voice and almost see her in his mind. He was about eight years old, and she had walked with him up to McManemin's store. He stood by as she paid three cents for three peppermint sticks. But Mr. McManemin handed him four candy sticks.

Once out of the store and well down the road home, John spoke up. "Hey, Mama, look! Mr. Ed gave me four peppermint sticks. Ain't that great?"

"No, son. That's stealing."

"It ain't stealing, Mama! He gave them to me. He has lots of them. It don't matter, and he won't even know."

His mom stopped, put her hands on his small shoulders, and they shared a connection that he never forgot.

"Son, listen to that voice in your heart. Sometimes, you must be really quiet so you can hear it, but it's always there. If it doesn't feel right, it's not."

He remembered the two of them walking back to that store and how afraid he was that Mr. Ed would be mad. He wasn't. He laughed, told John how much he admired an honest kid and proved it by letting him keep the extra candy.

As that memory and illusion left his mind, he picked up his son and walked into his house.

* * *

On a Friday at 7:50 a.m., he picked up his last paycheck and turned in his cleaner.

"Al, I'm done. This is not the job for me."

"John, you're a natural. Take a few weeks off and come back and see us."

"No. I'm finished with the Stratton Cleaner business."

When that last paycheck ran low, John briefly thought about the good money that was likely available if he showed up at the Stratton office.

But somewhere, deep inside, he could hear that small, still voice: *Doing what is right is not always the easy way out, but it does allow you to sleep at night.*

John found a job where a paycheck came every Friday and was based on the work he did that week. He needed the structure and the satisfaction of an honest job. He tried out a number of jobs, from working in the butcher shop of a local grocery store to a couple of manufacturing situations.

He learned to focus on goals for his family and to strike a balance between work and leisure to the benefit of his family. He and Ruth were married for twelve years, had three wonderful sons, but they eventually grew in different directions.

They were children when they married and were grateful for the time together. As adults, they realized each had a different path to follow. They divorced but remained friends.

Within a few years, John met and married his current spouse. Together they created a butane gas delivery service. John made the deliveries, and Becky kept the records. It was a job that allowed the management control John needed, along with the public interaction he enjoyed.

The peace that passes all understanding is ready and waiting for anyone willing to make the effort to study and to listen to that small, still voice of conscience, of God, of love and saving Grace.

www.ingramcontent.com/pod-product-compliance
Lightning Source LLC
LaVergne TN
LVHW010704110826
845149LV00014B/3222

* 9 7 9 8 9 9 2 0 0 9 3 2 3 *